SONG LEADING

W. Hines Sims

Secretary, Church Music Department
Baptist Sunday School Board

CONVENTION PRESS
Nashville, Tennessee

© 1959 • CONVENTION PRESS
Nashville, Tennessee

5119-16

Church Study Course for Teaching and Training
This book is number 1916 in category 19, section for
Young People and Adults

Library of Congress Catalog Card Number: 59-6204
Printed in the United States of America
5.MH646

Contents

Church Study Course

THE CHURCH STUDY COURSE began October 1, 1959. It is a merger of three courses previously promoted by the Sunday School Board—the Sunday School Training Course, the Graded Training Union Study Course, and the Church Music Training Course. On October 1, 1961, the Woman's Missionary Union principles and methods studies were added.

The course is fully graded. The system of awards provides a series of five diplomas of twenty books each for Adults or Young People, two diplomas of five books each for Intermediates, and two diplomas of five books each for Juniors.

The course is comprehensive, with books grouped into twenty categories. The purpose of the course is to help Christians to grow in knowledge and conviction, to help them to grow toward maturity in Christian character and competence for service, to encourage them to participate worthily as workers in their churches, and to develop leaders for all phases of church life and work.

The Church Study Course is promoted by the Baptist Sunday School Board, 127 Ninth Avenue, North, Nashville, Tennessee 37203, through its Sunday School, Training Union, Church Music, and Church Administration departments; and the Woman's Missionary Union, 600 North Twentieth Street, Birmingham, Alabama 35203; and by the respective departments in the states affiliated with the Southern Baptist Convention. A complete description of the course and the system of awards may be found in the leaflet, "Trained Workmen," which may be obtained without charge from any one of these departments.

A record of all awards earned should be maintained in each church. A person should be designated by the church to keep the files. Forms for such records may be ordered from any Baptist Book Store.

REQUIREMENTS FOR CREDIT IN CLASS OR HOME STUDY

If credit is desired for the study of this book in a class or by home study the following requirements must be met:

I. IN CLASSWORK

1. The class must meet a minimum of seven and one-half clock hours. The required time does not include assembly periods. Ten class periods of forty-five minutes each are recommended. (If laboratory or clinical work is desired in specialized or technical courses, this requirement may be met by six clock hours of classwork and three clock hours of supervised laboratory or clinical work.)

2. A class member who attends all class sessions and completes the reading of the book within a week following the last class session will not be required to do any written work for credit.

3. A class member who is absent from one or more sessions must answer the questions (pp. 122-23) on all chapters he misses. In such a case, he must turn in his paper within a week, and he must certify that he has read the book.

4. The teacher should request an award for himself. A person who teaches a book in the section for Intermediates or Juniors (any category) or conducts an approved unit of instruction for Nursery, Beginner, or Primary children will be granted an award in category 11, Special Studies, which will count as an elective on his own diploma. He should specify in his request the name of the book taught or the unit conducted for Nursery, Beginner, or Primary children.

5. The teacher should complete the Request for Book Awards—Class Study (Form 150) and forward it within two weeks after the completion of the class to the Church Study Course Awards Office, 127 Ninth Avenue, North, Nashville, Tennessee 37203.

II. IN HOME STUDY

1. A person who does not attend any class session may receive credit by answering all questions for written work as indicated in the book. When a person turns in his paper on home study, he must certify that he has read the book.

2. Students may find profit in studying the text together, but individual papers are required. Carbon copies or duplicates in any form cannot be accepted.

3. Home study work papers may be graded by the pastor or a person designated by him, or they may be sent to the Church Study Course Awards Office for grading. The form Request for Book Awards—Home Study (Form 151), must be used in requesting awards. It should be mailed to Church Study Course Awards Office, 127 Ninth Avenue, North, Nashville, Tennessee 37203.

III. CREDIT FOR THIS BOOK

This book is number 1916 in category 19, section for Young People and Adults.

W. HINES SIMS
Secretary, Church Music Department
Baptist Sunday School Board

About the Author

W. Hines Sims is a native of Louisiana. He attended the public schools of Texas, completing high school at Mart, Texas. He graduated from Hardin-Simmons University, Centenary College, and George Peabody College. He has done graduate work at Southwestern Baptist Theological Seminary, University of Nebraska, Northwestern University, and Peabody College. He holds the following degrees: A.B., B. Mus., M.A., Mus. D., and attended Peabody College on a Ph.D. fellowship.

Dr. Sims has had extensive experience in both the public schools and churches of Arkansas, Nebraska, Louisiana, and Tennessee. He served as minister of music, Queensboro Baptist Church, Shreveport, Louisiana, 1935-45, and held a similar position with the First Baptist Church, Nashville, Tennessee, 1945-47. The excellency of his work has always been recognized and has afforded him preparation for the position he now holds as secretary of the Church Music Department of the Baptist Sunday School Board.

He has had wide experience as a director of church music conferences, clinics, schools, and choral organizations throughout the Southern Baptist Convention. In his present position he gives guidance to a comprehensive music education program, which includes publication, curriculum development, and field promotion for more than 33,000 churches of the Convention. He serves as director of the Southern Baptist Music Leadership Conferences at Ridgecrest, North Carolina, and Glorieta, New Mexico. He is the author of numerous articles and pamphlets dealing with various phases of the church Music Ministry and of three books, *Instrumental Music in the Church* (Broadman Press), *Song Leading* and *Church Music Manual* (Convention Press). The last serves as a basic guide for the development of a comprehensive Music Ministry in our churches.

Dr. Sims has served as compiler and editor of several hymnals and choral collections published by Broadman Press. He is editor in chief of *The Church Musician* and editor of *Baptist Hymnal*, released in March, 1956, by Convention Press.

How to Use This Book

Congregational singing is an integral part of the church Music Ministry. In many ways it is perhaps the most important music activity of the church, since it is a portion of the service in which each worshiper *can* and *should* participate.

Why is it that congregational singing in many churches is dynamic and expressive, while in others it is listless and lifeless, often lacking in fervor, quality, and power? Is it that one church congregation is made up of people, who, individually and collectively, are trained vocalists, while in another church such training is nil? It is true that some churches have better singing than others—in the worship services, in department assemblies, and wherever people express the "joy of their salvation" through song. It is quite unlikely that any church ever had a complement of singers, with each one a trained vocalist in his own right.

What, then, is the answer? Most frequently the quality of singing is, in a sense, a "mirroring" of the leader—his interests, enthusiasm, experience, training, and determination to master the art of leading songs.

Congregational singing, as well as all worship participation, is a privilege which the people are to share in, not something that musicians do *for* them, thereby placing them in the role of listeners. Much, therefore, depends on the song leader and his readiness to take advantage of every opportunity for improvement in fulfilling his responsibility.

Song leading is an art within itself. There are many excellent, well-trained musicians who are "masters" of this skill. There are also many technically "amateur" musicians who effectively serve their churches in the capacity of song leaders. Both the *trained* and the *untrained* benefit personally through such service, but, best of all, each can be a blessing to his church and those who gather to worship from time to time. This book sets forth the basic principles of song leading. It has been prepared primarily for training volunteer song leaders. With application and determination one can learn the fundamentals of directing without benefit of extensive training in music.

Many persons will have opportunity to study this text in regularly scheduled class sessions, under the guidance of a competent, qualified teacher. Such classes will usually be a part of the training activities as promoted in the local church, associational, state, or Convention-wide level. The Church Study Course for Teaching and Training is explained on page vi. Requirements for credit in either the class or home study plan are discussed on page vii.

There are various methods of studying this book, either individually or collectively. The following plans are suggested:

1. Some elected song leaders may find it necessary to pursue the home study plan. This is explained on page vii. They may wish to follow also this routine study in addition to class participation. In carefully following the suggestions, "For Further Study," at the close of each chapter, the student will gain a great deal of experience; the additional studies will afford him a wider acquaintance with many hymns he will use in discharging his duties.

   He will find it helpful to secure a set of the Broadman Conducting Charts (26b) for use in home study.

2. Several song leaders from a local church or from a group of churches may wish to form a class, meeting weekly under the guidance of a qualified teacher, and continue such a class for the period of time necessary to cover the material and complete requirements for credit.

3. Many ministers of music schedule regular monthly music workers' conferences for all song leaders and pianists of the church. Materials in the text, *Hymn Playing*, and in this book, Song Leading, can be used as a basis for general discussion, or they may be studied in detail, extending the study over a period of several months.

4. A song leader and a pianist, as a team, may wish to pursue a systematic study of the material in these two texts, considering the various points of study as they apply to their respective responsibilities.

5. There is great need for the church pianist to understand the basic principles of conducting; therefore, a class in song leading, promoted exclusively for church pianists, is worthy of consideration.

6. It is suggested that a person, after completing the study of this book, continue to use it as a manual for regular study and practice. A systematic plan for the study of all conducting patterns, supplementary hymns, and exercises suggested for further practice will provide the serious student with a variety of materials with which to improve his present skills.

These suggestions are only a few of the possible approaches to studying Song Leading. More material has purposely been included in this book than can be thoroughly studied in seven and one-half hours of class time. Each teacher must, therefore, determine the specific needs of his class. He will formulate his teaching procedures accordingly.

The person desiring to become proficient in song leading should set aside some time each day for studying and practicing the hymns he is to direct. By following a consistent schedule of preparation and combining the basic principles of song leading and interpretation as set forth in this text with the wealth of additional fine hymn literature found in a standard hymnal, any leader can increase his technical facility and, therefore, be able to render more effective service to his church.

LOREN R. WILLIAMS
Editor, Church Music Materials
Church Music Department
Baptist Sunday School Board

CHAPTER 1 OUTLINE

    I. UNIFORMITY IN CONDUCTING

        1. Conducting Is Universal

        2. Song Leading

        3. Preparation for Leading

    II. BEING A LEADER

        1. Dress and Manner

        2. Enthusiasm and Sincerity

        3. Musicianship and Imagination

        4. Technique and Style

1
Approach to Song Leading

It has been well said that music is the universal language. And, indeed it is. It appeals to all mankind, knowing no nationality, race, creed, or boundary. It is a friend to all men everywhere. Its dwelling place is the human heart.

The most natural expression of music is singing. Since earliest recorded history, men have used their voices to sing praises to their Creator and to express their thanksgiving to him. The human voice is the world's first and most magnificent instrument. It has the means of expressing joy, sorrow, exultation, pathos, praise, prayer, and an infinite number of other emotions and characteristics.

All who manifest an interest in music soon come in contact with the great hymns and songs of the ages. They sing them in worship, in the educational organizations of the church, in revivals, in homes, at work, and in other walks and areas of life. A song in the heart quickly finds vocal expression on the lips.

I. UNIFORMITY IN CONDUCTING

1. *Conducting Is Universal*

Just as music is universal, even so is the technique of conducting. Throughout the years, the patterns indicating beats, rhythm, measure, expression, phrasing, and flow of music have been standardized. Any conductor who stands before a great chorus, orchestra, congregation, or even a small group can use standard conducting patterns and be understood the world around. A good conductor need not know the language of the people he is conducting. When he knows the music, those before whom he stands will understand his sign language. Conducting is therefore a means whereby the leader expresses, through the movement of his hands, the expression of his face, eyes, body motion, and various gestures, the interpretation of the music which he wishes to convey to those producing it. Conducting is simply a sign language that is universal and is understood by those who sing or play the music.

2. *Song Leading*

It is entirely possible that most people who are interested in music and accustomed to singing will sooner or later be asked to lead a group in singing. Particularly is this true in church activities. A young person who manifests an interest in singing and in music will probably be elected as song leader in a department. Where shall he begin? What should he do in order to lead the people in singing?

The leading of music, as related to hymns and gospel songs that are used in group singing, is a form of conducting. Song leading employs the basic elements of conducting. It is not necessary that one have as extensive training or be as well grounded in music as is the professional conductor in order to lead singing.

It is important that a song leader realize that he must lead, not follow. His leading must be done in a confident and graceful manner and in such a way as to assure the people that he knows what he is doing. Song leading is more than arm waving. It is an exact science which can be applied with grace, smoothness, and appeal.

There is a great need for song leaders in all churches and communities. Occasionally, one may hear statements to the effect that it is not necessary to have a song leader in order to get people to sing. Nothing could be more misleading. There are perhaps a few people who will sing spontaneously or from a sense of duty, but it is very difficult to get a congregation to sing with spirit, understanding, and precision without the leadership of a capable song leader. One may very well reason that if a symphony orchestra or a great chorus must be directed by a professional conductor, how much more necessary it is to have a leader for people who are inexperienced as singers and musicians. Group singing invariably improves under the direction of a fine song leader.

3. *Preparation for Leading*

If a person is to become successful in leading people to sing, he must develop a style and an understanding of what he is trying to do. He should become acquainted with music fundamentals, basic conducting patterns, music interpretation, and the best methods of encouraging people to sing. He must cultivate the ability to lead people in singing. Knowledge of song leading comes only through a willingness to study and to discipline oneself in practice and application of the principles involved.

It is the purpose of this text to present some of the basic principles of song leading and to interpret them in such a way that they can become a tool in the hands of any individual desiring to lead singing. The emphasis will be placed on hymns and songs for use in church activities. Through practice and application of these basic principles, one should be able to become a reasonably competent leader of singing.

Foremost in preparing to lead and in becoming a leader of singing is a willingness to accept the responsibility. Dependability is a prime virtue for every person who would lead a group. One should work to develop a smooth style, a pleasing approach, and a poise that puts him at ease before the people he is to lead. Also important is a willingness to plan worship programs with the worship leaders, to practice with the accompanist and special singers, and to approach leadership responsibilities in an optimistic and cheerful manner which reflects a readiness and eagerness to do the very best he can to lead people to enjoy good congregational singing.

We would encourage each person, therefore, who begins the study of this text to resolve at the outset that he will be willing not only to master all of the patterns, but to practice each song faithfully and to develop his leadership ability in all of the important areas which contribute to success. Song leading must be smooth and graceful. The singers must realize that their leader is not laboriously struggling through a song, but is leading with confidence, ease, grace, and magnetic appeal which encourage good participation.

II. BEING A LEADER

1. *Dress and Manner*

If one would be a successful leader, he must present a pleasing appearance before the group he is to lead. At all times he should be well groomed, conservative in attire, and as neat as possible. He should do his best to appeal to those whom he is to direct. His best will require diligent work in the development of a pleasing voice, correct posture, personal magnetism, and a radiant personality. It is necessary that he divest himself of any mannerisms which would be distracting. People will not respond to the leadership of one who is loud, brassy, critical, and ill-mannered. On the other hand, his first appearance before a group should draw its immediate and favorable attention. His evident authority as a leader will inspire the people to sing.

2. *Enthusiasm and Sincerity*

Natural enthusiasm is a blessing. Forced enthusiasm, which is an evident attempt to be enthusiastic just to impress a group, is devastating. The successful song leader will have both enthusiasm and sincerity, which will attract the interest of all who are before him. By enthusiasm we do not mean the exuberance of a cheerleader or a circus clown, nor do we mean that sincerity is always expressed in seriousness and extreme gravity. We think of natural enthusiasm as that which is found in an optimistic and buoyant approach, marked by a sense of humor, kindliness, gentleness, a natural feeling of correctness, and an effervescence of spirit. Sincerity becomes evident when the audience recognizes that the leader is confident in his approach, is intent upon what he is doing, and wants to help them sing. Only then can the song service become a meaningful experience for the leader and for the people. They realize that he is enjoying what he is doing and that he wants them to receive the blessings he enjoys.

In developing enthusiasm and sincerity, a song leader never does anything that would discourage people in their singing, but he does everything possible to help them sing and worship together. A

3

song leader never chides or ridicules the singers, or criticizes the singing of the people he leads. On the contrary, he encourages, compliments, and helps them in their singing. He will be buoyant, yet modest, sympathetic, helpful, and truly sincere in all that he tries to do to serve those whom he leads.

3. *Musicianship and Imagination*

Obviously, if one is to lead music he must know something about it. Unless a leader has an understanding of the basic principles of leading and a knowledge of the music he is to lead, he cannot expect an audience to follow or respect his leadership. Always, the song leader must know his music perfectly. He must understand music and reflect this understanding in his leading. It is well that he memorize the song he is to lead and that he understand its message and content. He will thus be able to interpret it to the people. In speaking of music leaders, one great conductor said, "It is better to have the song in your head than to have your head in the song." Certainly this is true, and if one would lead successfully he should know his music well and understand its meaning so that he will be able to interpret it to the people and have them follow his leadership.

The words of a song constitute its most important element. Music is merely the vehicle in which the words ride. The leader must be musician enough to interpret the song and to direct it so that all the people will receive the message in their hearts and heads and be able to appreciate its full meaning. The better the leader's musicianship, the better are his possibilities of comprehending his work and of being able to interpret the music to those under his leadership.

Parallel with musicianship is imagination. And, imagination must be used in the selection of the songs for each occasion. It must be used in interpreting the songs if their full message is to be presented; and it must be used in a way that will create enthusiasm on the part of the singers and help them understand what they are singing. Imagination and musicianship team together in helping to make one a successful leader of singing.

4. *Technique and Style*

A song leader, if he is to be successful, cultivates his technical facility, developing a free and easy style that reflects naturalness and ease. In order to acquire such technique and style, one must practice diligently. As practice progresses, one develops a mastery of standard song leading patterns and employs them in a graceful and easy manner so that the people can understand them. The leader thus is able to lead with natural ease because he becomes a part of the song. He interprets the song in all of its meaning.

In order to acquire good technique and good style, it is essential for one to develop complete naturalness in all that he does before the

4

audience. This will mean clarity in announcing the number, the use of devices in creating interest in the song, and the planning of the songs in a way that will promote a continuing interest in what is being done. Good planning will result in the logical sequence of songs chosen and in the development of balance and "rightness" in the song service.

In announcing a song, one must do it with clarity and forcefulness. It is most helpful to use some device which will activate an interest in the song as the number is announced. For example, it is not of particular interest to the congregation or group for the leader to say, "Everybody get a book and turn to number 269." Yet how many song leaders begin in such a manner! Would it not be better to make a preliminary statement, such as, "This morning we are singing some great hymns of assurance. One of the best loved is Fanny Crosby's 'Blessed Assurance, Jesus Is Mine.' If you will please turn to number 269, we shall stand together and sing all of the stanzas." It is not necessary to go into a long dissertation concerning any song, but it is helpful to say just a few words which will arouse the interest of the group.

It is also well for the leader to convey his wishes to the congregation. Are the people to sit or stand for this particular song? Are they to sing all of the stanzas, or will one or more stanzas be omitted? Are other instructions necessary for clarity of procedure? It is well for the song leader to say to the congregation exactly what he wants them to do. If they are to sing only certain stanzas, they should be told which ones to sing. If they are to stand during the song, they should know that they are to stand. It is possible for the song leader to say in a very few words exactly what he wants a congregation to do. He can develop an interest in the song by stating in a simple manner those things that will help the congregation sing with ease, assurance, and confidence.

The song leader's manner and attitude will also help activate an interest in the song. The expression on his face should be pleasant, reflecting an air of anticipation of wonderful singing. An expressionless face and a draggy manner do not encourage any group to sing. One must interpret the spirit of the song. A joyous song, such as "Joy to the World! The Lord Is Come," should be directed with joy permeating every movement and expression. Too many song leaders fail at this point. Their faces are expressionless, eyes dull and downcast, posture poor, body movements sluggish. They give the general impression that song leading is a tiresome task. They are actually trying to lead "Joy to the World! The Lord Is Come," while their face, hands, and body movements say they are leading "Hark from the Tomb, a Doleful Sound!" A song leader must reflect the spirit of the song, leading it in an appealing and convincing manner.

It is best that one lead as simply as is possible. In using the standard patterns of song leading, it is unnecessary to have a great many flourishes and meaningless motions. Always, the length of the stroke of the hand and arm should be in accord with the dynamic level desired. The softer the music, the shorter the conducting strokes should be;

5

the louder the music, the longer the strokes. Also to be considered is the size of the group the song leader is to lead. He would use strokes of greater length and sweep before a congregation of a thousand people than before a group of fifty. Each motion of the hand is made for a purpose. As the various aspects of the different conducting patterns and strokes are developed, we shall discuss the meaning of each motion and the best way to use it.

It is important that we realize that the song leader uses his hands, arms, eyes, face, lips, brows, voice, and body movements to lead in a capable, attractive, appealing, and proficient manner. By using these various means, he becomes naturally expressive of the flow of music as he tries to interpret the true meaning of the song to the congregation.

FOR FURTHER STUDY

1. Try to observe several different song leaders in action. Evaluate their work as related to the suggestions in this chapter.

2. Study the Topical Index of *Baptist Hymnal*, observing its organization. Develop a song service based on each of the following subjects: consecration, faith, grace, Christmas (Christ—Birth of), and Easter (Christ—Resurrection of).

3. Consult the Index of Authors, Translators, and Sources of Hymns in *Baptist Hymnal*. Who wrote the greatest number of hymns in the hymnal? How many authors have only one hymn included? Two? Three?

4. Study the lives of Ira D. Sankey and Homer Rodeheaver. Name some factors that contributed to their success.

CHAPTER 2 OUTLINE

I. NATURE OF MUSIC

    1. Rhythm

    2. Melody

    3. Harmony

II. BASIC STRUCTURE OF SONGS

    1. Song Divided into Measures

    2. Note and Rest Values

    3. Time Signature

    4. Key Signature

    5. Accented and Unaccented Beats

III. PRINCIPLES OF DIRECTING

    1. Direction of Beats

    2. Position

    3. Patterns

    4. Tempo

    5. Practice

    6. Practice with Accompanist

    7. Accompanists Should Study Song Leading

    8. Song Leaders Should Study Accompanying

2
Some Basic Principles of Leading

I. NATURE OF MUSIC

1. *Rhythm*

Music is made up of three basic elements—rhythm, melody, and harmony. We hear steady rhythm in the ticking of a clock. Each tick may be called a beat. Rhythm in music is the pulsation which gives regularity of beats and duration of sound as the music flows along. As we listen to music we will observe that some of the beats are strong and others are weak; some are accented and others are unaccented. In studying a song and in singing it, we usually find the strong beats on the more important words and the weak beats on the less important words.

2. *Melody*

The melody is the tune. A beautiful, flowing melody is much to be desired in all music. In songs which we shall be conducting, the melody is very important, but the flow of the rhythm and the harmony also contribute to the beauty of the song. We are all accustomed to following the melody, but as we become song leaders we must be aware that the melody is supported by the rhythmic structure and the harmonic structure. In directing a song, we are to establish a balance between rhythm, melody, and harmony and bring out the characteristics of each, blending them into a beautiful rendition.

3. *Harmony*

Harmony deals with the blending of the various voice parts into chord structures. Although a melody flows in a horizontal direction, the harmony flows in a vertical direction. Thus, in a chord we usually find the melody note most frequently assigned to the soprano and generally three other notes which are given the alto, tenor, and bass. Sounded simultaneously, they produce a very pleasing chord. In leading singing, we try to encourage not only good melodic singing (horizontal flow), but also good part singing (vertical flow), and a leader must be able to hear and sense the chord structures as well as the melodic and rhythmic flow.

II. Basic Structure of Songs

1. *Song Divided into Measures*

As stated earlier, the song leader must have a knowledge of music that will enable him to interpret it to the people he is to lead. To acquire such a knowledge, he must study basic theory, conducting, and music interpretation. Since we are studying some of the fundamental factors in song leading and are preparing to engage in actual conducting, we shall illustrate some of the things necessary for putting music on paper.

(1) All music is written on a staff of five lines and four spaces.

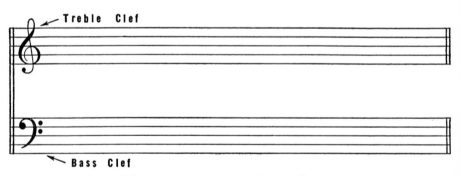

Illus. 1. STAFF

(2) Women sing the music written on the top staff of a song and men sing the music written on the bottom staff. The treble clef ($\oint$) is used by the women; the bass clef ($\mathcal{9}$:) by the men. The two staffs together form the grand staff.

Treble Clef

Bass Clef

Illus. 2. CLEFS AND GRAND STAFF

(3) A song is divided into measures. A measure is simply a grouping of accented and unaccented beats within a space between vertical lines across the staff. These lines are called measure bars. A measure may have two beats, three beats, four beats, or more in its length. Some of the beats are strong, and some are weak, but always without fail, the first beat in each measure is a strong or accented beat. The illustration here shows four measures on the staff. In most hymns, there are four measures for each phrase of the poem. At the end of the illustration is a double bar which usually occurs only at the end of a song.

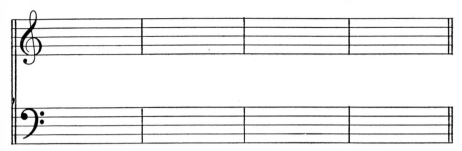

Illus. 3. MEASURES AND BARS

2. *Note and Rest Values*

All music is divided into notes and rests of certain values. A note in music indicates a length of sound. A rest indicates a length of silence. The note values most commonly used in church music are: whole note, half note, quarter note, sixteenth note, and thirty-second note. Observe the chart giving the comparative note and rest values.

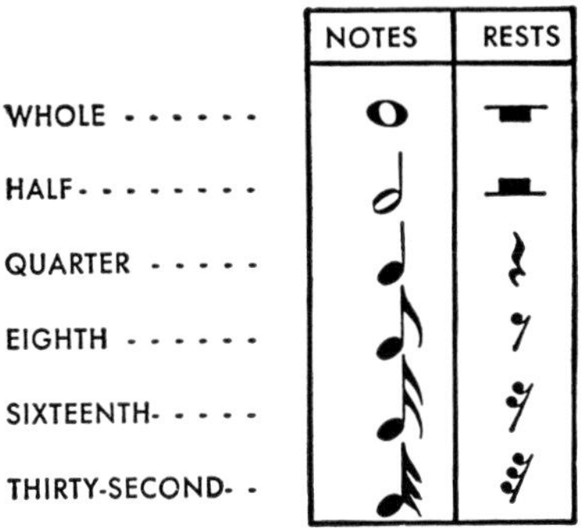

	NOTES	RESTS
WHOLE · · · · · ·	o	▬
HALF · · · · · · · ·	♩	▬
QUARTER · · · · ·	♩	ξ
EIGHTH · · · · · ·	♪	𝄾
SIXTEENTH · · · · ·	♬	𝄿
THIRTY-SECOND · ·	♬	𝄿

A whole note can be divided into two half notes. A half note can be divided into two quarter notes. A quarter note can be divided into two eighth notes. An eighth note can be divided into two sixteenth notes, and so on. Any note may be divided into smaller segments.

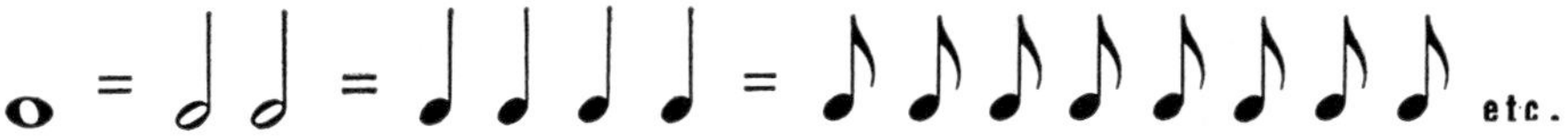

Illus. 4. NOTE VALUES

What has been said concerning notes applies equally to rests. The rest values most commonly used in church music are: whole rest, half rest, quarter rest, sixteenth rest, and thirty-second rest.

11

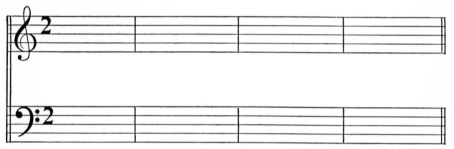

Illus. 5. Rest Values

3. *Time Signature*

If you will look at the beginning of a song you will see some figures. There will be a top figure and a bottom figure much like the numerator and denominator of a fraction. These figures are called the "time signature" of the song. The top figure always indicates the number of beats in each of the measures. The bottom number always indicates the type of note receiving one beat. Thus, if the top number is 2, there are two beats to each measure. If the top number is 3, there are three beats to each measure. If the top number is 4, there are four beats to each measure, and so on.

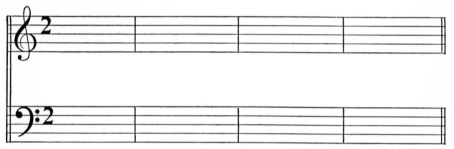

Illus. 6. Designation of Beats to Each Measure

If we should change the numeral *2* to 3 in Illustration 6, there would be three beats to each measure; a change to 4 would indicate four beats to each measure, etc.

Understanding top numeral values, as presented in Illustration 6, we are able to understand the bottom number in our time signature. If the bottom number, therefore, is 2, a half note is the basic beat note of each measure; if the bottom number is 4, a quarter note is the basic beat note, etc. Illustration 7 says simply that there are two half notes

As written:　　　　　　　　　　　**Could be written:**

Illus. 7. Two Half Notes to Each Measure

to each measure. Illustration 8 says there are three quarter notes to each measure.

Illus. 8. THREE QUARTER NOTES TO EACH MEASURE

Thus, the number of beats and the types of notes and rests contained in any song will be governed by the time signature.

4. *Key Signature*

Immediately following the time signature at the beginning of a song is the key signature. This is indicated by the number of sharps or flats used, or by the absence of sharps and flats, in which case the key is "natural." Since key signatures are intimately related to theory, we shall not discuss them here, but refer the student to another text, *The Beginning Music Reader* by James C. McKinney, in the Church Study Course for Teaching and Training. It is important for the song leader to know key signatures and to be able to read a song; otherwise, he will experience difficulty in trying to lead. It is strongly recommended that all song leaders not only master the various conducting patterns, but that they also become proficient in sight reading in any key.

5. *Accented and Unaccented Beats*

We have stated previously that a measure contains both accented and unaccented beats. Some are strong, and others are weak. However, the strong beats and the weak beats of a measure always occur in identical relationship to one another.

In a measure of 2/4 time, beat 1 is strong and beat 2 is weak. In counting, we emphasize the first beat: *1*, 2, *1*, 2, etc.

In 3/4 time, beat 1 is strong; beats 2 and 3 are weak. We count *1*, 2, 3; *1*, 2, 3, etc.

All time signatures are multiples or combinations of two beats or three beats to a measure. Thus, four beats to a measure would simply double the two-beat measure, and be counted *1*, 2, *3*, 4. Six beats to a measure would double the three-beat measure. Counting, we would say *1*, 2, 3, *4*, 5, 6. However, in doubling the two-beat and the three-beat measures to make four and six beats, the beats added become a secondary grouping and receive not quite so strong an accent.

13

A table showing the time signatures and strong and weak beats will therefore be helpful at this juncture. The student is encouraged to memorize the table.

Beats	Time Signatures			Accents			
2 in a measure	2	2	2				
(duple)	2	4	8	1 strong	2 weak		
3 in a measure	3	3	3	1 strong	2 weak	3 weak	
(triple)	2	4	8				
4 in a measure	4	4	4	1 strong	2 weak		
(quadruple)	2	4	8	3 medium	4 weak		
6 in a measure		6	6	1 strong	2 weak	3 weak	
(sextuple)		4	8	4 medium	5 weak	6 weak	
(compound duple)							
9 in a measure		9	9	1 strong	2 weak	3 weak	
(compound triple)		4	8	4 medium	5 weak	6 weak	
				7 medium	8 weak	9 weak	
12 in a measure		12	12	1 strong	2 weak	3 weak	
(compound quadruple)		4	8	4 medium	5 weak	6 weak	
				7 medium	8 weak	9 weak	
				10 medium	11 weak	12 weak	

Illus. 9. TABLE OF TIME SIGNATURES

III. PRINCIPLES OF DIRECTING

1. *Direction of Beats*

Throughout this text, all diagrams and instructions are presented on the basis of the leader's directing with his right hand. A left-handed student who prefers to use his left hand for indicating the patterns will reverse the diagrams and instructions relative to rhythm and expression. The hand conducting the patterns will be referred to as the *lead* hand, while the other will be the *expression* hand.

The number of beats to a measure determines the direction the hand and arm will take in describing the various patterns which rep-

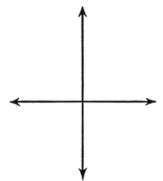

Illus. 10. FIELD OF BEATING

resent the rhythm. Each rhythm has a different pattern which may be modified according to the expression to be used—whether loud, soft, smooth or marked, or simply nonexpressive. The movements of the hand are down, up, left, right, and their various combinations.

Shown here is what we call the "field of beating." Generally speaking, its extremes reach a height of several inches above shoulder level, downward to about the hips, left for about fifteen inches, and right as far as an arm's length. Smaller beats diminish these distances proportionately.

This field of beating, which encompasses the areas of motion of the right hand and arm, will be presented in conjunction with future illustrations of beat patterns as dotted lines. Thus, it will be possible for the student to better understand beat positions and beat relationships.

2. *Position*

It is important, in directing, that one stand erect, that weight be evenly distributed on the feet, and that the body feel absolute balance and freedom. The feet are slightly apart. The arms are perfectly free for easy movement, and one feels comfortably positioned. The head is up, shoulders are back, and the eyes are looking at the group. Leaning back too far or forward too much will throw one off balance. The knees should be somewhat firm, but neither stiff nor relaxed. The entire body feels free and easy. The hands and arms are ready for action.

In using the hand to conduct, or lead, the arm is extended from the shoulder, the hand is stretched outward in a natural easy position. The fingers are extended quite naturally without being curled in or held out in a stiff, uncomfortable looking position. It is as if one would extend his hand to shake hands with a friend, except that he raises his hand shoulder high, with his arm outstretched. The palm is turned in and slightly downward.

In preparing to conduct, one takes the stance described and raises his hand to shoulder height. In so doing, he gains the position of "attention." He then begins with a preparatory beat which he gives prior to the first beat of the song. If the song starts on the first (down) beat of a measure, the preparatory beat will be an upstroke with the value of one beat, which is used to indicate the tempo (speed) at which the song will be sung and also to indicate to the group that singing is now to begin on the downbeat. The term is just what it says—the preparatory beat—giving time for breath intake by the group and for readiness. The hand and arm go up and then come down on the downstroke, indicating beat 1, at which time the singing actually begins.

The accompanying diagram shows the preparatory beat. Practice this several times in rhythm by saying, "Beat, down," accenting the word, "down."

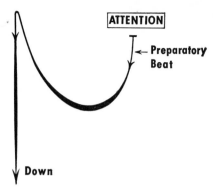

Illus. 11. PREPARATORY BEAT

We shall discuss preparatory beats more fully a bit later. At present, let us make a mental note that such a beat always precedes the actual beginning of a song. The *direction* of this preparatory beat is determined by the beat upon which the first note of the song begins. The preparatory beat is always given in rhythm and is combined with the first beat to establish the tempo, mood, and style in which the song is to be sung.

3. *Patterns*

As stated earlier, the first beat in each measure is always an accented beat. Furthermore, it is always what we call a *downbeat*. Thus, the conducting patterns always call for a downbeat for the first beat in any measure. The other beats in the measure are definite in their position and relation to the first beat.

(1) *Two-beat measure.*—A two-beat measure (often called duple measure) is expressed by a *downbeat* of the hand for *1* and an upbeat for 2. Having only two beats, the first being *down* and accented, causes us to reason that the *last* beat must be *up* and unaccented in order to be in position for the next downbeat. The hand therefore in a two-beat measure begins the motion with a preparatory beat and continues by going down for 1 and up for 2. The direction is thus:

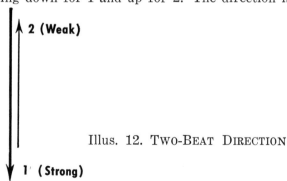

Illus. 12. TWO-BEAT DIRECTION

Practice the two-beat measure many times while counting aloud *down*, up, *down*, up: and then *1*, 2, *1*, 2, *1*, 2, etc. Accent 1 by speaking quite loudly and follow it by gently speaking the 2. This procedure is designed to help one acquire the feeling of definite strength in the first beat of *each measure*. Also, since *1* is the only downbeat in conducting, any singer or instrumentalist watching a director can easily identify the first beat of each measure. Individuals who have rests in their parts may easily count the measures and come in at the exact moment their music begins. Or, should one lose his place, he may readily find it by watching the downbeat of the director.

(2) *Three-beat measure.*—We have learned already that the first beat of a measure is always *down* and the last beat of a measure is always *up*. In two-beat measure, a simple down-up beat is all that is necessary. In three-beat measure (often called triple measure), we know 1 is down and 3 is up. Consequently, we place 2 in a position to the outside, thus contributing to ease in following it with beat 3. Therefore, we use a triangular shape—down, out, up—to accomplish our design. Generally it would appear:

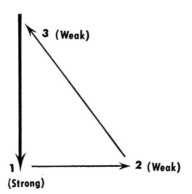

Illus. 13. THREE-BEAT DIRECTION

Practice this many times, first counting aloud *down*, out, up, *down*, out, up; then *1*, 2, 3, *1*, 2, 3, etc.

(3) *Four-beat measure.*—Remembering that the first beat is down and the last beat is up in any measure, we know that in a four-beat measure (often called quadruple measure), 1 will be down and four will have to be up. Thus, beats 2 and 3 must go—one in and the other out—before going to the upbeat on *four*. Our pattern would therefore be *down*, in, *out*, up. Recalling also that four-beat measure is double the two-beat measure, we remember our accents. Consequently, beat 1 will be strong, beat 2, weak, beat 3 relatively strong, and beat 4 weak. The pattern would take a form somewhat like this:

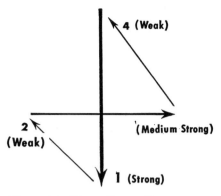

Illus. 14. FOUR-BEAT DIRECTION

Practice many times, first speaking aloud, *down,* in, *out,* up, *down,* in, *out,* up; then *1,* 2, *3,* 4, *1,* 2, *3,* 4, etc.

4. *Tempo*

Tempo means speed. Along with correct patterns, accents, and style, it is important that a song leader understand the tempo at which a song is to be sung. Tempo can very well be determined by reading carefully the words and ascertaining the song's nature and meaning. If it is a martial type of tune, it will doubtless move faster than one of a strictly devotional nature. The words of the song suggest the tempo. The nature of the music also helps determine the speed at which it will be sung. One would not lead "Have Thine Own Way, Lord" at the same tempo and in the same conducting style that he would use in a song such as "Onward, Christian Soldiers." The two songs are different in style and in nature and therefore require a different approach in conducting. One would require a smooth, expressive beat; the other would be rather vigorous and marked in its flow.

One learns correct tempo through experience. We have all heard songs sung too fast or too slow. Frequently, when a song is sung faster than its true tempo would indicate, the words lose some of their effectiveness, and there is lack of unity in the singing of the people. Some singers fail to keep up with the tempo, and others resent a fast tempo because they have been accustomed to singing at the proper speed. Singing a song at too slow a tempo is equally ineffective. Always it is desirable that the song leader set the right tempo for the song in order to convey to the congregation the true meaning of the message. The ability to establish correct tempo comes from experience, a knowledge of traditional speeds, and a close study of the song and its nature and content. By studying and memorizing the songs, the leader will be able to develop the tempo which is best suited for each.

5. *Practice*

Just as an organist or pianist cannot hope to develop facility at the keyboard without practice, neither can a person hope to develop facility as a song leader without diligent and adequate practice. Practice is indispensable in developing any phase of music leadership or technical ability. It is suggested therefore that the song leader do a great deal of practicing before a full-length mirror if at all possible. He can do this in the privacy of a room at home, if one has a full-length mirror, or before a dressing table mirror which is large enough for one to see oneself as the audience would see him. Practicing before a mirror will not only develop gracefulness but will eliminate unnecessary flourishes, excessive beats, and mannerisms which are unattractive to a congregation. At the same time, one can develop grace, ease, and naturalness by studying his work in a mirror as he develops the conducting patterns.

6. *Practice with Accompanist*

Just as it is important to practice before a mirror, even so it is important to practice with an accompanist. The song leader and the accompanist work together as a team. The accompanist is supposed to follow the leader rather than the leader follow the accompanist. The song leader always sets the tempo and interprets the music while the accompanist watches him carefully and plays exactly as the leader conducts. A song leader and a pianist of a Sunday school department, therefore, practice the songs together. They plan their song services. The pianist practices the introduction of each hymn to be sung and knows exactly what to do in each instance. The song leader helps the pianist by indicating the tempo and something of the volume and expression most appropriate for the song.

The accompanist works with the song leader and tries to support the singing as much as possible. Therefore, he will employ a firm touch at the piano and a good basic rhythmic accompaniment. Good congregational singing progresses best with a solid, rhythmic accompaniment from the piano and a clear, decisive beat from the song leader.

In playing an introduction, the accompanist begins at the beginning of the song and plays about four measures in order to establish the tempo, the pitch, the rhythm, and the mood of the song. He is careful to end the brief introduction on the same full chord that is found at the beginning of the song.

7. *Accompanists Should Study Song Leading*

All through this course in song leading, the accompanist and the conductor work closely with each other, each supporting the efforts of the other. They work together also in the church. *It is just as important therefore that pianists and organists know conducting patterns and be able to lead singing as it is for a song leader to know the proper con-*

ducting patterns. All pianists and organists in the various departments of the church and those responsible for playing for church services should study conducting and master the various conducting patterns. They will then know what the conductor is doing when he is leading a song. It is also helpful for various members of the choir and members of the congregation to know something of basic conducting patterns so that they can better appreciate what the song leader is trying to do and be able to follow him more acceptably.

All song leaders and pianists of every department and organization of the church should try to master the various techniques, patterns, and suggestions given in this text in order that they may better serve their church and the groups with which they work. A good song leader is an indispensable person within the church and the various organizations. Since it is not difficult for one to learn to lead quite acceptably, there is little excuse for song leaders and accompanists' not knowing the basic principles of song leading. We would encourage every church to give frequent courses in song leading in order to develop the maximum number of competent leaders for service in all organizations.

8. *Song Leaders Should Study Accompanying*

Even as it is important for an accompanist to know conducting patterns and to be able to follow the song leaders with accuracy and precision, it is also important for the song leader to know something of the art of accompanying. He should know the type accompaniment best suited for particular situations and types of music. He should know how best to apply various techniques in accompanying to heighten the color and interpretation of the music and to provide more variety and interest. He should recognize that rhythmic flow, chord structures, phrasing, and interpretation are all affected by the style of accompanying as well as style of leading.

Being able to talk the language of an accompanist, to demonstrate what is needed and to express the fine points essential to producing a superior accompaniment for any music at any time are assets to be desired by every song leader.

Two books appearing in Category 19 of the Church Study Course for Teaching and Training under the titles of *Hymn Playing* by Loren R. Williams and *The Church Pianist* by Helen Midkiff will be of great value to any song leader desiring a greater understanding of accompanying.

FOR FURTHER STUDY

1. Make a study of *Baptist Hymnal*, observing the time signatures. How many hymns are written in duple measure? Triple measure? Quadruple measure? Compound measure?

2. Consult the book, *Beginning Music Reader*, by James C. McKinney. Name the key signatures for the flat keys. Name the sharp keys.

3. Make a check of all the pianos in your church. Is each one so placed as to enable the pianist to see the song leader with ease?

4. Practice duple, triple, and quadruple beat direction before your mirror, checking for ease of motion, flow, smoothness, naturalness, accented and unaccented beats.

CHAPTER 3 OUTLINE

    I. IMPORTANCE OF CLARITY

        1. Personal Approach

        2. Preparatory Beat

        3. Simple Diagram for Two-Beat Measure

    II. TWO-BEAT MEASURE IN 2/4 TIME

        1. Analyze the Song

        2. Attack and Release

        3. Consider the Accompanist

        4. Modified Two-Beat Measure

    III. TWO-BEAT MEASURE IN 2/2 TIME

        1. The Lead Hand and Volume

        2. The Expression Hand

        3. Dynamic Levels

3
Two-Beat Measure

I. IMPORTANCE OF CLARITY

All we have said in the two previous chapters is designed to contribute to the ease and clarity necessary to successful song leading. Unless a group can understand the "sign language" of the leader, it is not likely that there will develop the unity and spirit of freedom the singers should possess while singing.

It is essential that the song leader conduct with clarity, indicating tempo, dynamics, expression, flow, and phrasing. To do so, he must master the various rhythm patterns, know the music, and understand what each song requires in interpretation and precision.

1. *Personal Approach*

As the leader comes before the group that he is to lead, he should keep his head up and his eyes on the people, not down in the book. It is not good form to hold a hymnal in one hand, conduct with the other, and try to look at the hymnal and the people at the same time.

The leader, almost every time he leads, will be on a platform which has a pulpit or speaker's stand. The leader should place his hymnal on this stand, and take his position either directly behind it or slightly to the side. Both hands should be free—one for conducting the rhythm patterns and the other for indicating expression. If the stand is rather high and of solid construction, it is better that the leader stand slightly to one side so his lead hand may be seen easily by all the people. At no time should his conducting strokes be obscured by the stand. His stance should be balanced, his eyes up, his approach appealing, and his manner such as to encourage complete participation.

2. *Preparatory Beat*

In chapter 2, we introduced the use of the preparatory beat. (See Illus. 11.) The song leader should always use a preparatory beat to begin the singing. It is the beat that readies the singers and accompanist, sets the tempo, starts the movement of the song, indicates the mood, and establishes the pattern. Without it the singers and accompanist would be at a loss concerning these things and would experience difficulty in starting together.

The hand is extended and raised to about shoulder height and to the right of the shoulder line to a position we call "attention." The singers see the hand in the "attention" position and observe the director is ready to begin. Then he begins the preparatory beat, which has the value of one full beat and indicates that the singers are to begin singing in rhythm when the hand reaches the next beat. The preparatory beat is something like the signal used for beginning a race when the starter says in rhythm, "On your mark—get set—go!" The position of *attention* puts the singers "on their mark"; the *preparatory beat* "gets them set" with tempo, breath, mood, and dynamics, and the *first stroke* of the pattern says "Go." For a downbeat, the hand is held out at "attention," then it describes the arc of the preparatory beat to move down. In this illustration (and others to follow), the dotted lines represent the vertical and horizontal axes of the field of beating.

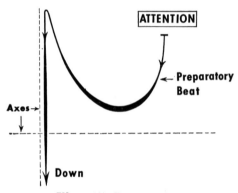

Illus. 15. DOWNBEAT

When the singing begins on the upbeat in a two-beat measure, we use somewhat of a reversed pattern for the preparatory beat. For "attention," the hand is held inward from that of the previous example, the preparatory beat goes outward, and singing begins on the *up*beat.

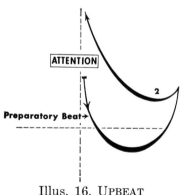

Illus. 16. UPBEAT

The student is urged to practice Illustrations 15 and 16 many times in order to be prepared for leading the songs which we shall soon be studying and leading.

3. Simple Diagram for Two-Beat Measure

It is quite difficult to draw an accurate diagram of the exact path and movements which the lead hand takes in conducting the various patterns. A slow tempo requires a movement different from that of a fast tempo. Music that is soft is conducted somewhat differently from that which is loud. Therefore, in the accompanying diagrams, the *direction* is the important thing.

Generally, as explained in Illustration 12, the simplest pattern for two-beat measure (2/8, 2/4, 2/2) is down and up. The right hand gives the preparatory beat and comes to a position directly in front of the right shoulder, then drives downward for the accented beat 1. Singing begins exactly on count 1 and continues, the first beat sounding until the count of 2, and 2 sounding until the coming of 1 again. The simplest two-beat diagram is the one following the vertical axis, going down and up in the same path with no rebound or other deviation. Practice Illustration 17 many times, speaking first DOWN, up, DOWN, up, then counting *1, 2, 1,* 2, etc. Accent the first beat.

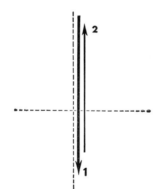

Illus. 17. TWO-BEAT PATTERN

II. TWO-BEAT MEASURE IN 2/4 TIME

1. Analyze the Song

As one looks at a song, he should see many things. First, there is the title. This is usually the first line of the hymn, or it may be a descriptive title telling something of the content of the song. For example, "We Have Heard the Joyful Sound" also goes by the title of "Jesus Saves." Both the first line and the title are given in the alphabetical index of *Baptist Hymnal.*

Second, immediately under the title we usually find the tune name. This name usually has some significance. It may indicate a place or an event in the life of the author or composer, or it may be the actual name of either. The tune name gives identity when more than one tune is used with a set of words. For example, "All Hail the Power of Jesus' Name" appears three times in *Baptist Hymnal* with different tunes, "Coronation," "Miles Lane," and "Diadem."

Third, we see some numbers or letters following the tune name. These give the number of syllables in each line or phrase of the song. The group of figures 8.6.8.6 (common meter) means that the first line of the poem has 8 syllables, the second line 6, the third line 8, and the last line 6. These numbers are referred to as the metrical structure of the song. Generally, an 8.6.8.6. (C.M.) poem can be sung to other 8.6.8.6 (C.M.) tunes.

Fourth, we look to the upper left side of the song for the name of the author or the source of the hymn poem. In *Baptist Hymnal*, dates are given for the author's birth and death.

Fifth, we find at the upper right of the song the name and dates of the composer or the source of the tune.

Sixth, we examine the song to determine the time signature, key signature, length, and the number and sequence of the stanzas. Occasionally, there are stanzas which may be omitted from the singing without impairing the message of the song, but there are many songs in which the message would be lost if any stanza should be omitted.

Before beginning to conduct, it is helpful for the leader to be aware of all these factors which go into the making of a song. A careful study of each song to be directed will give valuable information concerning its type, message, period, interpretation, and appropriateness for the occasion. Let us now consider our first song (Ex. 1, p. 27).

"Praise Him, All Ye Little Children"

Such a beat as is diagrammed in Illustration 17 may very well be used for a song that moves along at quite a lively tempo and contains no complications relating to phrasing or expression. One of the first songs we learn in Sunday school, as children, is simple in construction and may be directed with the downbeat pattern of Illustration 17. We observe there are two beats to each measure and a quarter note gets one beat. We also observe the first measure is a full measure and the first word is on the first beat. Get the attention of the singers with the "attention" gesture, use a preparatory beat to get started, and beat the song in a steady down-up rhythm.

2. *Attack and Release*

We have discussed the procedure for getting a song started. How do we get one stopped? The beginning of a song should always start with a clean and unified attack. This comes in Exercise 1, on the downbeat 1. As the leader's hand describes the preparatory beat and then comes down, all begin singing when the hand reaches the figure *1* at the bottom of the stroke.

Praise Him, All Ye Little Children

GOD IS LOVE. 10. 6. 10. 6.

Anonymous   Anonymous

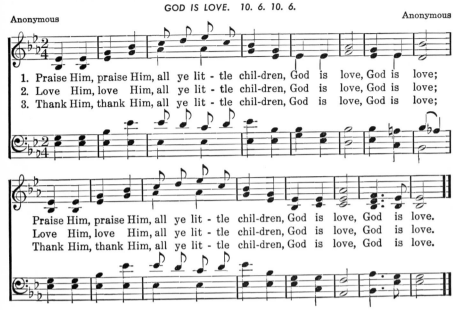

1. Praise Him, praise Him, all ye lit - tle chil-dren, God is love, God is love;
2. Love Him, love Him, all ye lit - tle chil-dren, God is love, God is love;
3. Thank Him, thank Him, all ye lit - tle chil-dren, God is love, God is love;

Praise Him, praise Him, all ye lit - tle chil-dren, God is love, God is love.
Love Him, love Him, all ye lit - tle chil-dren, God is love, God is love.
Thank Him, thank Him, all ye lit - tle chil-dren, God is love, God is love.

Singing continues throughout the song, the hand marking beat 1 with a downstroke and beat 2 with an upstroke. Then comes the last measure containing a half note. This half note has the value of two beats. For beat 1 the hand should go down, but instead of returning to the *up* position, let it describe instead an outward and upward arc to the position of "attention" and hold there during the completion of the two beats. This position enables the director to hold the note longer if he desires, or he may use the *release* or *cutoff* stroke in rhythm by bringing his hand diagonally across the front of his body at the end of count 2. This sharp movement, which is not in any pattern line, indicates to the singers that they are to release the tone together. The last measure would appear in diagram something like this:

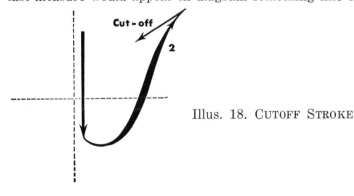

Illus. 18. CUTOFF STROKE

"Take My Life, and Let It Be," ("Hendon")

Similar to "Praise Him, All Ye Little Children," but a bit slower in tempo, is the song of personal consecration, "Take My Life, and Let It Be," as set to the tune, "Hendon." The same conducting stroke of down-up may be used on this song. As you lead it, strive for a smooth flow of the hand and a clean attack and release by the singers. Make sure they follow you as you lead. Observe that the song begins on a downbeat.

EXERCISE 2.

Take My Life, and Let It Be

HENDON. 7. 7. 7. 7. 7.

FRANCES R. HAVERGAL, 1836-1879

HENRI A. CESAR MALAN, 1787-1864

1. Take my life and let it be Con - se - crat - ed, Lord, to Thee; Take my hands and let them move At the im - pulse of Thy love, At the im - pulse of Thy love.
2. Take my feet and let them be Swift and beau - ti - ful for Thee; Take my voice and let me sing Al - ways, on - ly, for my King, Al - ways, on - ly, for my King.
3. Take my sil - ver and my gold, Not a mite would I with-hold; Take my mo - ments and my days, Let them flow in cease-less praise, Let them flow in cease-less praise.
4. Take my will and make it Thine, It shall be no long - er mine; Take my heart, it is Thine own, It shall be Thy roy - al throne, It shall be Thy roy - al throne. A - MEN.

3. Consider the Accompanist

It is advisable to work as much as possible with a competent accompanist. Discussing the songs with this musician and going over them thoroughly as to tempo and expression will help make the interpretation effective. If one is working with an accompanist in the practice of these songs, it may be desirable to have him play a brief introduction to each song. These discussions will give the accompanist an understanding of the tempo desired.

For the introduction, the director will stand erect, nod to the accompanist to begin, and await the completion of the brief introductory measures. The director then brings his hand to the position of "attention" at about the time the introduction is completed. He then gives the preparatory beat, and singing begins on the first word of the song.

Should the introduction played by the accompanist be faster or slower than the director desires, he will begin the song at exactly the tempo he wishes to use, and the accompanist will immediately accommodate his tempo to that of the director. So will the singers. At all times, the accompanist and the singers are to respond to the tempo and expression as set by the director. The song leader will make it a practice to encourage and help the accompanist as much as possible. Never should he criticize or find fault in public. Any comments or suggestions should be made in private. Any commendation should be expressed both in private and in public.

4. Modified Two-Beat Measure

The simple down-up beat of the first two songs is not entirely appropriate for every song in two-beat measure. Some songs have a slower tempo which calls for more expressive and easy-flowing beats. Others have subdivided beats that need the additional emphasis which can be given by making both beats 1 and 2 quite definite.

In directing the downbeat, there is a natural rebound which comes after the hand descends to 1. This rebound may well be utilized to lead into 2 which will follow the upbeat line as given in Illustration 17.

The diagram of this pattern would take a form somewhat like this:

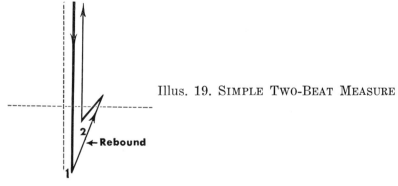

Illus. 19. SIMPLE TWO-BEAT MEASURE

Practice this pattern many times, counting *1, 2, 1, 2, 1, 2,* etc. As the hand strikes 1, there is a slight rebound upward and a bit outward, and then 2 is marked as the hand goes in slightly and upward. Illustration 19 may well be termed a non-expressive beat because it becomes the basic diagram from which we shall work for songs employing slower tempos, divided beats, and careful phrasing.

"Count Your Blessings"

The song, "Count Your Blessings," is so constructed that it requires a beat pattern as shown in Illustration 19. The eighth notes subdivide the basic beat of a quarter note and make necessary the marking of beat 1 *and* beat 2. Although the time signature indicates that there are two quarter notes to each measure, we readily observe that there are equivalent eighth notes in most of the measures. (Two eighth notes equal one quarter note.) Beat "Count Your Blessings" as illustrated in 19. Start on a downbeat. Have the singers sing with precision and clarity, enunciating each syllable clearly and emphasizing the message. EXERCISE 3.

Count Your Blessings

BLESSINGS. 11. 11. 11. 11. with Refrain

JOHNSON OATMAN, JR., 1856-1922   EDWIN O. EXCELL, 1851-1921

1. When up-on life's bil-lows you are tem-pest tossed, When you are dis-cour-aged, think-ing all is lost, Count your man-y bless-ings, name them one by one, And it will sur-prise you what the Lord hath done.
2. Are you ev-er bur-dened with a load of care? Does the cross seem heav-y you are called to bear? Count your man-y bless-ings, ev-'ry doubt will fly, And you will be sing-ing as the days go by.
3. When you look at oth-ers with their lands and gold, Think that Christ has prom-ised you His wealth un-told; Count your man-y bless-ings, mon-ey can-not buy Your re-ward in heav-en, nor your home on high.
4. So, a-mid the con-flict, whether great or small, Do not be dis-cour-aged, God is o-ver all; Count your man-y bless-ings, an-gels will at-tend, Help and com-fort give you to your jour-ney's end.

Count your bless-ings, name them one by one: Count your
Count your man - y bless - ings, name them one by one; Count your man - y

bless - ings, See what God hath done; Count your bless - ings,
bless - ings, see what God hath done; Count your man - y bless - ings,

rit. *a tempo*

name them one by one; Count your man - y bless-ings, see what God hath done.

"Loyalty to Christ"

What has been said concerning "Count Your Blessings" applies also to "Loyalty to Christ." The time signature indicates two quarter notes to each measure, but these are subdivided. An additional problem comes in the very first note which we call a "pickup" note. Study will reveal that it is the last half of count 2. To further explain it, the last measure of the song contains only one and one-half beats (count them); the last half of beat 2 has been separated from the last measure and placed at the beginning of the song. Composers follow such a procedure in order to establish a good metrical structure for the song, giving the principal beats to the principal words.

31

Loyalty to Christ

LAMBDIN. *Irregular with Refrain*

E. TAYLOR CASSEL, 1849-1930   FLORA H. CASSEL, 1852-1911

1. From o-ver hill and plain There comes the sig-nal strain, 'Tis loy-al-ty, loy-al-ty,
2. O hear, ye brave, the sound That moves the earth a-round, 'Tis loy-al-ty, loy-al-ty,
3. The strength of youth we lay At Je-sus' feet to-day, 'Tis loy-al-ty, loy-al-ty,

loy-al-ty to Christ; Its mu-sic rolls a-long, The hills take up the song,
loy-al-ty to Christ; A-rise to dare and do, Ring out the watch-word true,
loy-al-ty to Christ; His gos-pel we'll pro-claim Thro'-out the world's do-main,

REFRAIN

Of loy-al-ty, loy-al-ty, Yes, loy-al-ty to Christ. "On to vic-to-ry! On to

vic-to-ry!" Cries our great Commander: "On!" .... We'll move at His com-mand,
great Commander; "On!"

We'll soon pos-sess the land, Thro' loy-al-ty, loy-al-ty, Yes, loy-al-ty to Christ.

Since this song, "Loyalty to Christ," begins on the last half of the upbeat 2, we shall have to use a preparatory beat similar to that presented in Illustration 16. We beat down from about half as high as we would ordinarily, rebound into 2, and "pick up" the first note thus:

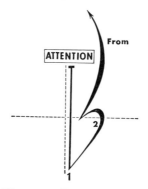

Illus. 20. Pickup Beat

As you prepare to conduct "Loyalty to Christ," make sure that the people you are leading are ready. The eyes, a look of expectation, and a clear-cut beat for the pickup will bring the desired results as you conduct, using the pattern of Illustration 19.

III. Two-Beat Measure in 2/2 Time

1. *The Lead Hand and Volume*

We have already pointed out the necessity for studying each song so that one may become permeated with its message, meaning, and interpretation. In following this procedure, a song leader increases his ability to discern the correct tempo, volume, phrasing, and general sweep of the song as the melody rises and falls in peaks and valleys of loudness and softness.

The lead hand, beating the rhythm, will indicate a louder phrase by increasing the size of the beat and by moving outward from the body. As the music becomes softer, the hand will so indicate by shortened strokes and a movement toward the body. Simply stated, the beat becomes larger for an increase in volume and smaller for a decrease. As the beat becomes larger, the hand naturally moves farther from the body; as it becomes smaller it moves toward the body. The size of the gesture then is in proportion to the volume desired.

"Here at Thy Table, Lord"

A careful study of the song, "Here at Thy Table, Lord" (Ex. 5), will reveal that its subject is the Lord's Supper and that it is devotional in nature. It calls therefore for a smoothly flowing, expressive beat. The song leader would beat it in a pattern void of sharp angles and quick movements. A smooth preparatory beat would ready the singers and indicate that the song is to be sung in a smooth, sustained, and easy-flowing manner. The pattern would open up more than in Illustration 19, assuming more flow through elimination of "points" in the beats. Although it is difficult to show by illustration exactly the path the hand will follow, it would look something like this:

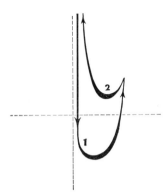

Illus. 21. MODIFIED TWO-BEAT MEASURE

Study of the accompanying diagram (Illus. 21) will reveal that *direction* of the beats has not changed. The two-beat measure is still down-up. However, in order to gain smoothness for a slower and more even-flowing song, such as "Here at Thy Table, Lord," as in contrast to "Count Your Blessings," the leader *broadens* and rounds off the rebound stroke in order to convey the idea of sustained tonal continuity going into beat 2 and continuing into beat 1 of the following measure.

As one studies the song, he recognizes that the first eight measures call for only a moderate stroke, neither too short nor too long. Average volume is all that is desired. At the beginning of measure 9, the leader begins increasing the stroke length in order to build a gradual climax to be reached at the beginning of measure 12. The downbeat of 12 is rather dynamic and intense, indicating the peak of volume. Following this climax, the beats gradually become smaller and return to average in the last two measures. The last measure is conducted with a beat which moves down, out, and up for 2 to the position of "attention," from which the cutoff stroke is given. (See Illus. 18.)

2. *The Expression Hand*

The left hand is usually the expression hand. A person using his left hand as the lead would use his right hand to indicate expression. The leader uses the expression hand to indicate volume and to develop phrasing and expression in co-ordination with the lead hand. When he lifts the expression hand, palm up, volume is increased. Intensity of volume may range from very soft when the hand is lowered to hip level—palm down, to very loud when the hand and arm are stretched out full length to a few inches above shoulder level—palm up. From this position, in order to diminish volume, the leader slowly turns the

Here at Thy Table, Lord

BREAD OF LIFE. 6. 4. 6. 4. D.

MAY P. HOYT   WILLIAM F. SHERWIN, 1826-1888

1. Here at Thy ta - ble, Lord, This sa - cred hour, O let us
2. Come then, O ho - ly Christ, Feed us, we pray; Touch with Thy

feel Thee near, In lov - ing pow'r; Call - ing our thoughts a - way
pierc - ed hand Each com - mon day, Mak - ing this earth - ly life

From self and sin, As to Thy ban-quet hall We en - ter in.
Full of Thy grace, Till in the home of heav'n We find our place. A-MEN.

hand over, palm toward the congregation, and lowers the arm gradually. He holds the expression hand up for *loud,* down for *soft.* Moving the hand upward with the palm up increases volume; moving the hand downward with the palm down decreases volume.

"Jesus Shall Reign Where'er the Sun"

Let us now experiment with the expression hand alone. The hymn, "Jesus Shall Reign Where'er the Sun," has numerous ascending and descending passages. To get the feel of using the expression hand for volume, leave the lead hand at the side for a while and practice using the expression hand alone. Begin the song with the expression hand extended, palm up, slightly above hip level. Now sing the hymn while gradually lifting the hand, step by step and note by note, until the hand is extended outward, shoulder height, by the time you begin the third measure. A peak of volume is reached at M.3 (measure 3). Now, turn the hand over and move it downward slightly while singing M.3 and 4. The volume remains about the same in M.5 and 6 and then diminishes in M.7 and 8. For the remainder of the song, the hand will follow the rise and fall of the melody line. Increased volume is indicated for ascending notes and decreased volume for descending notes.

No doubt you will feel awkward using the expression hand, at the beginning of this exercise, but experiment freely and practice faithfully with this hand alone while singing "Jesus Shall Reign Where'er the Sun" numerous times.

EXERCISE 6.

Jesus Shall Reign Where'er the Sun

DUKE STREET. L. M.

Isaac Watts, 1674-1748   John Hatton, d. 1793

1. Je - sus shall reign wher - e'er the sun Does his suc-
2. From north to south the princ - es meet To pay their
3. To Him shall end - less pray'r be made, And end - less
4. Peo - ple and realms of ev - 'ry tongue Dwell on His

ces - sive jour - neys run; His king-dom spread from shore to shore,
hom - age at His feet; While west-ern em - pires own their Lord,
prais - es crown His head; His name like sweet per - fume shall rise
love with sweet-est song, And in - fant voic - es shall pro - claim

Till moons shall wax and wane no more.
And sav - age tribes at - tend His word.
With ev - 'ry morn - ing sac - ri - fice.
Their ear - ly bless - ings on His name. A - MEN.

36

Following the practice of expression hand alone on Exercise 6, let the hand remain at the side and practice conducting with the lead hand, using stroke lengths to indicate volume increases and decreases as in Exercise 5. When you have mastered the lead-hand conducting pattern (Illus. 21), try using the two hands together. It is probable that you will experience both awkwardness and a lack of co-ordination. Do not let this bother you in the least—try again and again!

" 'Tis Midnight and on Olive's Brow"

This hymn is very expressive and should be sung smoothly and reverently. The leader will conduct it gently and gracefully with expressive beats, such as those shown in Illustration 21. Because the first note is a two-beat note, the preparatory beat will take the form of Illustration 16.

EXERCISE 7.

'Tis Midnight and on Olive's Brow
OLIVE'S BROW. L. M.

WILLIAM B. TAPPAN, 1794-1849   WILLIAM B. BRADBURY, 1816-1868

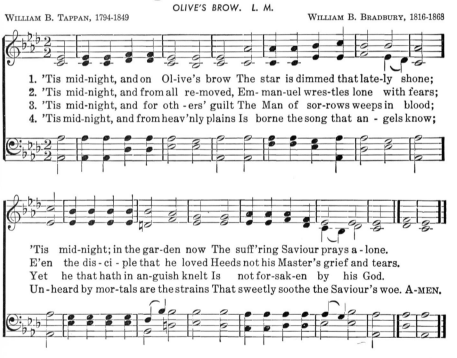

1. 'Tis mid-night, and on Ol-ive's brow The star is dimmed that late-ly shone;
2. 'Tis mid-night, and from all re-moved, Em- man-uel wres-tles lone with fears;
3. 'Tis mid-night, and for oth -ers' guilt The Man of sor-rows weeps in blood;
4. 'Tis mid-night, and from heav'nly plains Is borne the song that an - gels know;

'Tis   mid-night; in the gar-den now The suff'ring Saviour prays a-lone.
E'en   the dis-ci-ple that he loved Heeds not his Master's grief and tears.
Yet   he that hath in an-guish knelt Is   not for-sak-en by his God.
Un-heard by mor-tals are the strains That sweetly soothe the Saviour's woe. A-MEN.

3. Dynamic Levels

We have mentioned three ways in which the rise and fall of the volume of a song may be indicated.

    (1) Change the size of the beat.

    (2) Move the lead hand farther from or nearer to the body.

    (3) Use the expression hand.

37

EXERCISE 8.

Let All Mortal Flesh Keep Silence

PICARDY. 8. 7. 8. 7. 8. 7.

From the *Liturgy of St. James*
Trans. by GERARD MOULTRIE, 1829-1885

French Traditional Carol

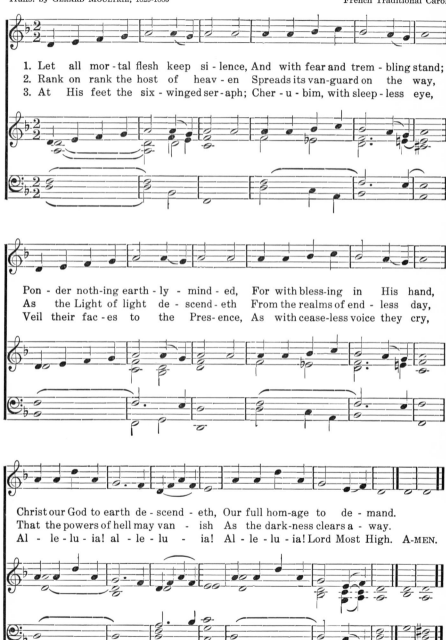

1. Let all mor-tal flesh keep si-lence, And with fear and trem-bling stand;
2. Rank on rank the host of heav-en Spreads its van-guard on the way,
3. At His feet the six-winged ser-aph; Cher-u-bim, with sleep-less eye,

Pon-der noth-ing earth-ly-mind-ed, For with bless-ing in His hand,
As the Light of light de-scend-eth From the realms of end-less day,
Veil their fac-es to the Pres-ence, As with cease-less voice they cry,

Christ our God to earth de-scend-eth, Our full hom-age to de-mand.
That the powers of hell may van-ish As the dark-ness clears a-way.
Al-le-lu-ia! al-le-lu-ia! Al-le-lu-ia! Lord Most High. A-MEN.

The song leader will utilize all three of these devices in developing his technique. As he practices he will develop freedom in both hands and be able to indicate the desired dynamic levels in the songs he will be leading. Learning to co-ordinate these three ways of controlling volume and intensity calls for practice and more practice. There is no other way to learn to lead. Correct practice makes perfect.

"Let All Mortal Flesh Keep Silence"

This old French carol, written in the minor key, is highly expressive. It is suggested therefore that the student study it carefully in order to understand its mood and expressive qualities. Understanding these, the student is requested to work out his own dynamic levels which he will follow. He is also to work out movements of the lead and expression hands. The student is "on his own" for this hymn and should work diligently on it for the purpose of developing his individual technique and expression.

FOR FURTHER STUDY

Practice the following duple-measure hymns:

Now to the Lord a Noble Song

Joy to the World! The Lord Is Come

Saviour, Breathe an Evening Blessing

Ride On! Ride On in Majesty!

Pentecostal Power

CHAPTER 4 OUTLINE

4
Three-Beat Measure

I. DIAGRAM FOR THREE-BEAT MEASURE

1. *Explanation of Diagram*

In chapter 2 we emphasized the importance of accented and un-accented beats. It is well that we recall the fact that all measures are divided into strong beats and weak beats. In the two-beat measure which we have just studied the accent is on beat 1. Beat 2 is weak or unaccented. In three-beat measure, the accent is on beat 1; beats 2 and 3 are unaccented or weak. The three-beat time signatures are 3/8, 3/4, and 3/2. We shall use the 3/4 and 3/2 for our examples. Reference to Illustration 13 will reveal the general direction the beats take in a three-beat measure (sometimes called triple measure). A right triangle is the general shape which the beats describe. Practice Illustration 13 several times while saying, "DOWN, out, up, DOWN, out, up"; then "*1*, 2, 3, *1*, 2, 3," etc.

In actual practice, the lead hand rebounds on beat 1 because it is an accented beat and is *down*. On the rebound the hand moves upward and then takes a direction outward, away from the body. This motion enables the singer to see beat 2 more easily than if the hand moved horizontally inward across the front of the body. Beat 2 leads naturally into beat 3, which, while being to the side of the body, returns inward and upward, progressing to the point where the downbeat for 1 begins again. The diagram for three-beat measure therefore takes this general shape:

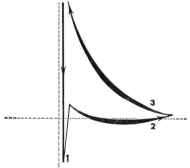

Illus. 22. SIMPLE THREE-BEAT MEASURE

Practice Illustration 22 many times while counting out the various beats, remembering always to accent downbeat 1.

2. *Songs in 3/4 Measure*

"Come, Thou Almighty King"
This hymn of adoration and praise should be led in a somewhat vigorous manner, beat 1 in each measure being accented. The song begins on a *downbeat*, having a full measure at the beginning. There are three beats to each measure, as indicated by the top number 3, and a quarter note gets one beat, as indicated by the bottom number 4 in the *time signature*. As you lead, remember the length of a stroke and its relationship to volume.

EXERCISE 9.

Come, Thou Almighty King

ITALIAN HYMN (TRINITY). *6. 6. 4. 6. 6. 6. 4.*

Anonymous

FELICE DE GIARDINI, 1716-1796

1. Come, Thou Al - might - y King, Help us Thy name to sing,
2. Come, Thou In - car - nate Word, Gird on Thy might - y sword,
3. Come, Ho - ly Com - fort - er, Thy sa - cred wit - ness bear,
4. To Thee, great One in Three, The high - est prais - es be,

Help us to praise: Fa - ther! all - glo - ri - ous, O'er all vic - to - ri - ous,
Our prayer at-tend! Come, and Thy peo - ple bless, And give Thy word suc-cess:
In this glad hour! Thou, who al - might - y art, Now rule in ev - 'ry heart,
Hence ev - er-more; His sov-'reign maj - es - ty May we in glo - ry see,

Come, and reign o - ver us, An - cient of Days.
Spir - it of ho - li - ness, On us de - scend.
And ne'er from us de - part, Spir - it of pow'r.
And to e - ter - ni - ty Love and a - dore. A-MEN.

"O Worship the King"

A study of this song will reveal immediately a 3/4 time signature, such as we had in the preceding song, but it begins on beat 3 instead of beat 1. Therefore, we shall use the preparatory stroke as presented in Illustration 16 because the hymn begins on an upbeat. Thus, we come to the position of "attention" with the lead hand raised about shoulder height and in line with the shoulder. Then we count 1 mentally, bring the hand down and out on 2 for the preparatory beat, and bring the singers in by gesturing toward them slightly on count 3, indicating they are to begin singing on this upbeat.

EXERCISE 10.

O Worship the King

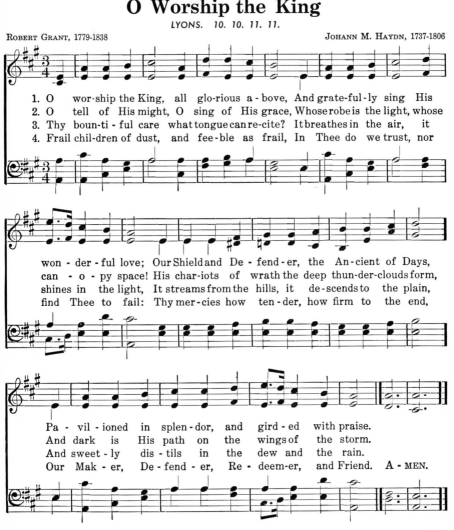

This hymn offers a fine opportunity for using the expression hand to build the volume, particularly in the last four measures of the second score and toward the end. Study the contour of the melody and the meaning of the words, and you will see great opportunity for developing contrast.

"I Love Thee"

This song also begins on beat 3 of the measure. Therefore, it will be necessary to use an outward preparatory beat to bring the singers in on the upbeat. Study of the song will reveal many opportunities for variety in expression.

EXERCISE 11.

I Love Thee

I LOVE THEE. 11. 11. 11. 11.

Anonymous

INGALL'S *Christian Harmony*, 1805

But how much I love Thee my ac - tions will show.
With Je - sus and an - gels and kin - dred so dear.
Thy grace shall in - spire both my heart and my tongue.
While riv - ers of pleas - ure my spir - it shall cheer. A - MEN.

3. *Beginning on Beat 2*

A song may begin on any beat of a measure. The determining factor is the rhythm of the music as related to the meter of the poem. In writing a hymn, the author uses the same metrical structure in each stanza. A composer, in setting a poem to music, gives emphasis to the important words and word syllables by use of the accented beats. Words and syllables not so important usually receive the unaccented beats.

The hold.—The composer uses many devices to emphasize a word or to create a special effect. One such device which is used quite frequently is the hold (⌒). Occasionally it is referred to as a *fermata, pause,* or *bird's eye.* Often it occurs over or under a note at the end of a phrase or at the end of a song, but it can be used almost anywhere to indicate emphasis.

In conducting a hold (⌒), the leader extends his hands and arms outward and upward and holds the note as long as he desires, disregarding generally the beat direction. Technically, a hold above a note doubles its value; practically, the tone lasts as long as the good judgment of the director dictates. The hold may end with a cut-off stroke.

"The Strife Is O'er"

In our next song we have two new problems. One is that it begins on beat 2, and the other is that it employs a hold at the end of the first line. As we study the song, we observe the presence of a *dal segno* (𝄋), which simply means that when the singers finish the first stanza, instead of returning to the beginning of the song, they will "return to the sign" (𝄋) for the second stanza and the other stanzas.

Careful study completed, and an understanding of the song developed, we are now ready to lead "The Strife Is O'er." To begin the song, the *down*beat will become the preparatory beat, and the singing will begin as the director gestures to the group to sing on beat 2. The downstroke will be shorter and without much accent, but beats 2 and 3 will receive emphasis. The downbeat of M.2 will receive considerable emphasis for two reasons: because it is an accented beat and because it falls on the principal syllable in "Al-le-*lu*-ia!" The expression hand

45

may be co-ordinated with the lead hand to give emphasis and increasing volume throughout the first score, the climax coming on the hold (⌢) at the end of the score.

The quarter rest following the hold should be indicated by an outward stroke because it follows a cutoff of the hold, and the upstroke will bring the singers in on beat 3. The rest occurring on beat 1,

EXERCISE 12.

The Strife Is O'er

VICTORY. 8. 8. 8. 4. with Alleluias

Authorship Uncertain
Tr. by FRANCIS POTT, 1832-1909

GIOVANNI P. DA PALESTRINA, 1525-1594
Adapted by WILLIAM H. MONK, 1823-1889

Al - le - lu - ia! al - le - lu - ia! al - le - lu - ia!

1. The strife is o'er, the bat - tle done;
2. The powers of death have done their worst,
3. The three sad days have quick - ly sped,
4. Lord, by the stripes which wound - ed Thee,

The vic - to - ry of life is won; The song of
But Christ their le - gions hath dis - persed; Let shouts of
He ris - es glo - rious from the dead; All glo - ry
From death's dread sting Thy ser - vants free, That we may

tri - umph has be - gun: Al - le - lu - ia!
ho - ly joy out - burst: Al - le - lu - ia!
to our ris - en Head: Al - le - lu - ia!
live and sing to Thee: Al - le - lu - ia! A - MEN.

46

three measures from the end, will receive a downbeat with not quite so much accent as usual, but beats 2 and 3 will receive emphasis. This song requires careful study, but it is a wonderfully effective and meaningful hymn on the resurrection when ably directed.

II. Modified Diagram for Three-Beat Measure

In discussing two-beat measure, we referred to the necessity for using a rather angular and precise beat on some songs and more of a smoothly flowing and rounded beat on other songs. The same is true of songs of three, four, or more beats. Some songs are rather marked in their rhythmic structure, and others are more sustained and connected in their flow.

It is expected of the leader that he indicate, through his conducting beats and patterns, exactly the effect he desires. There are some songs which may even be staccato, in which case, each conducting beat will be sharp and precise, clicking into each count without flow or flourish.

Understanding the necessity for variety, but at the same time realizing that the *direction* of the beats remains constant, we present a modified diagram of three-beat measure, which may best be used for the *legato* style of singing.

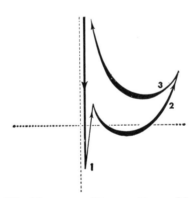

Illus. 23. Modified Three-Beat Measure

"The Head That Once Was Crowned"

This hymn is stately in structure and glorious in its message on the resurrection and exaltation of the Saviour. It should be studied carefully to let its message become meaningful through expressive conducting. Written in 3/2 measure, it begins on the upbeat. The director will use an outward preparatory beat and gesture to the singers to begin on the upbeat. The song should be sung with great earnestness and joyous thanksgiving.

The Head That Once Was Crowned

AZMON. C. M.

Thomas Kelly, 1769-1855

Carl G. Glaser, 1784-1829
Arr. by Lowell Mason, 1792-1872

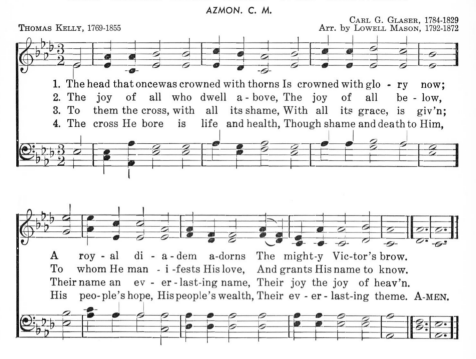

1. The head that once was crowned with thorns Is crowned with glo - ry now;
2. The joy of all who dwell a - bove, The joy of all be - low,
3. To them the cross, with all its shame, With all its grace, is giv'n;
4. The cross He bore is life and health, Though shame and death to Him,

A roy - al di - a - dem a-dorns The might-y Vic-tor's brow.
To whom He man - i -fests His love, And grants His name to know.
Their name an ev - er - last-ing name, Their joy the joy of heav'n.
His peo-ple's hope, His people's wealth, Their ev - er - last-ing theme. A-MEN.

"This Is the Day the Lord Hath Made"

Written in 3/2 measure and beginning on the upbeat, this hymn should be sung with precision and enthusiasm. The correct singing will call for a beat of clarity and precision and a tempo that moves fast enough to bring out a joyous expression of the hymn. The hold (⌒) at the end of the first line is simple because it is on beat 2. Let the hand move outward and continue to move slowly in order to lengthen the note to the desired effect; then bring the hand in and upward on the upbeat, which begins the next phrase.

"Jesus Calls Us o'er the Tumult"

A hymn of consecration, such as this, usually calls for an expressive beat. It is a hymn of decision which should be directed with smoothness, yet with a definite movement. It must not drag but move in such a manner as to urge decision on the part of the singer or listener. It, too, has a divided measure, beginning on the upbeat. Use the outward preparatory beat and bring the singers in on the third beat.

EXERCISE 14.

This Is the Day the Lord Hath Made

ARLINGTON. C. M.

Isaac Watts, 1674-1748

Thomas A. Arne, 1710-1778

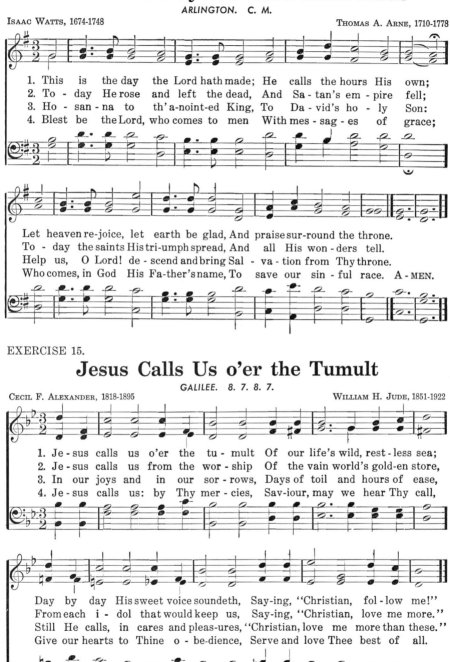

1. This   is   the day   the Lord hath made;   He   calls the hours His   own;
2. To - day He rose   and left the dead,   And   Sa - tan's em - pire   fell;
3. Ho - san - na to   th'a-noint-ed King,   To   Da - vid's ho - ly   Son:
4. Blest be   the Lord, who comes to men   With mes - sag - es   of   grace;

Let heaven re-joice, let   earth be glad, And   praise sur-round the throne.
To - day the saints His tri-umph spread, And   all   His won - ders tell.
Help us,   O Lord! de - scend and bring Sal - va - tion from Thy throne.
Who comes, in God   His Fa-ther's name, To   save our   sin - ful race.   A - MEN.

EXERCISE 15.

Jesus Calls Us o'er the Tumult

GALILEE.   8. 7. 8. 7.

Cecil F. Alexander, 1818-1895

William H. Jude, 1851-1922

1. Je - sus calls us o'er   the   tu - mult   Of   our life's wild, rest - less sea;
2. Je - sus calls us from the wor - ship   Of   the vain world's gold-en store,
3. In our joys and   in   our sor - rows,   Days of toil   and hours of   ease,
4. Je - sus calls us: by   Thy mer - cies,   Sav-iour, may we hear Thy call,

Day   by   day His sweet voice soundeth,   Say-ing, "Christian,   fol - low me!"
From each i - dol that would keep us,   Say-ing, "Christian,   love me more."
Still He calls, in cares and pleas-ures, "Christian, love   me more than these."
Give our hearts to Thine o - be-dience,   Serve and love Thee best of   all.

"O Happy Day That Fixed My Choice"

Careful study of this hymn will reveal that practically every measure in the song has the same rhythmic structure—a dotted half note followed by three quarter notes. The exceptions come only at the beginning of the refrain and the beginning of the last score. In conducting the song, the leader will begin on the last half of count 2. It will be advisable in this case to give a short downbeat for 1, let the hand move to the right for 2, and lift it slightly as a gesture to the singers to begin on the last half of 2. This gesture subdivides beat 2, and then the director will mark count 3 with precision as he goes on to 1. Diagrammed, the motion would look something like this:

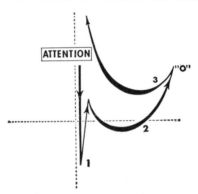

Illus. 24. PICKUP BEAT

Because of the metrical structure of "O Happy Day That Fixed My Choice" and because of its rather unusual beginning, the student will want to practice many times the "pickup" notes at the beginning as well as the measure rhythms while using the accompanying pattern as an example.

FOR FURTHER STUDY

Practice the following triple-measure hymns:

Praise to the Lord, the Almighty

Safely Through Another Week

To God Be the Glory

Immortal, Invisible

Great Is Thy Faithfulness

EXERCISE 16.

O Happy Day That Fixed My Choice

HAPPY DAY. L. M. with Refrain

PHILIP DODDRIDGE, 1702-1751

Adapted from EDWARD F. RIMBAULT, 1816-1876

1. O hap-py day that fixed my choice On Thee, my Sav-iour and my God!
2. 'Tis done–the great trans-ac-tion's done; I am my Lord's, and He is mine;
3. Now rest, my long-di-vid-ed heart, Fixed on this bliss-ful cen-ter, rest;
4. High heav'n that hears the sol-emn vow, That vow re-newed shall dai-ly hear;

Well may this glow-ing heart re-joice, And tell its rap-tures all a-broad.
He drew me and I fol-lowed on, Re-joiced to own the call di-vine.
Here have I found a no-bler part, Here heav'nly pleas-ures fill my breast.
Till in life's lat-est hour I bow, And bless, in death, a bond so dear.

REFRAIN

Hap-py day, hap-py day, When Je-sus washed my sins a-way!

He taught me how to watch and pray, And live re-joic-ing ev-'ry day;

Hap-py day, hap-py day, When Je-sus washed my sins a-way! A-MEN.

CHAPTER 5 OUTLINE

5
Four-Beat Measure

I. SIMPLE DIAGRAM FOR FOUR-BEAT MEASURE

A careful perusal of *Baptist Hymnal* will reveal more hymns written in four-beat measure than in any other. This time signature is employed most frequently and is often referred to as "common" time. In instrumental music the symbol "C" is often used instead of the figures 4/4. Most hymns of four-beat measure have the figures 4/4 or 4/2 in the time signature. Occasionally, one will see 4/8, but such a signature is rare. For our study we want to consider those four-beat measures in general use, namely, 4/4 and 4/2.

1. *Explanation of Diagram*

Earlier, the statement was made that the first beat of any measure is always *down* and accented. Also, we stated that a four-beat measure equals the doubling of a two-beat measure; therefore, the accented beats in four-beat measure are 1 and 3, and the unaccented beats are 2 and 4. Thus, we count *1*, 2, *3*, 4; *1*, 2, *3*, 4, etc. In a four-beat measure, however, the second accent, which comes on 3, is not so strong as the accent on 1. We refer to it as a secondary accent. For illustration, if we could weigh the beats of a four-beat measure, the first might weigh ten pounds, the second six pounds, the third eight pounds, and the last, five pounds.

Recognizing our accents and knowing that the first beat is always *down* and the last beat is always *up* in any measure, we place 2 and 3 in position to the left and right respectively, in order to utilize the strong and weak beats of four-beat measure to the best advantage. Thus our diagram would take the form of DOWN, in, OUT, up. A preliminary introduction to this pattern was rehearsed in Illustration 14. A simple four-beat diagram, without expressive motions, would be similar to Illustration 25. Practice it numerous times, first speaking DOWN, in, OUT, up; then *1*, 2, *3*, 4, etc. Accent 1 and 3, the *down*stroke and the *out*stroke (p. 54).

2. *Songs in 4/4 Measure*

"Angels, from the Realms of Glory"

For our first song of four-beat measure we want to use "Angels,

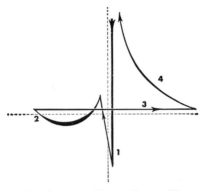

Illus. 25. SIMPLE FOUR-BEAT MEASURE

from the Realms of Glory." It is marked 4/4 with four beats in each measure and with a quarter note as the basic beat note. The song should be conducted with an enthusiasm indicative of the joy which is expressed in singing of the birth of Jesus. We use the pattern of Illustration 25. Since it begins on the downbeat, give a clear-cut preparatory beat and bring the singers in as the hand reaches the bottom of the beat. The expression hand may be employed to build a climax, particularly in the last score.

"God of Our Fathers, Whose Almighty Hand" (Ex. 18)

This stirring hymn has tremendous potential for moving expression. The director may use both hands to indicate strong rhythmic flow and dynamic levels. To begin the song, the director should turn to the accompanist and conduct the first two measures, indicating the sharp staccato of M.2 with sharp, direct beats that click into each count with precision. On the upbeat of M.2 he will look to the singers and bring them in with an accent on the word "God," the first note in M.3.

The first four measures should be sung with medium volume and precise pronunciation, the next four somewhat louder, the third four quite loudly. The volume climax will be reached at the beginning of the last four measures. The expression hand can help sustain the volume and intensity, particularly at the end of each phrase, by being lifted, palm up, during the three counts of the dotted half note. It can also emphasize the accent of beat 1 of the first measure in each phrase by being thrust directly forward, palm up, while the lead hand descends on the accented downbeat.

Study this song and master the variety in color, dynamic contrast, rhythmic movement, and intensity of message. It is a hymn well worth knowing and singing and should be a joy to conduct. The two-measure trumpet effect should be used and conducted before each stanza.

EXERCISE 17.

Angels, from the Realms of Glory

REGENT SQUARE. 8. 7. 8. 7. 8. 7.

JAMES MONTGOMERY, 1771-1854

HENRY SMART, 1813-1879

1. An - gels, from   the realms of   glo - ry, Wing your flight o'er
2. Shep-herds, in   the fields a - bid - ing, Watch-ing o'er your
3. Sag - es, leave your con - tem - pla - tions, Bright-er   vi - sions
4. Saints, be - fore   the   al - tar bend - ing, Watch-ing   long   in

all   the   earth; Ye   who sang cre - a - tion's sto - ry,
flocks by   night, God with man   is   now re - sid - ing,
beam a - far; Seek the great De - sire of na - tions,
hope and fear, Sud - den - ly the   Lord, de - scend - ing,

Now pro - claim Mes - si - ah's birth: Come and wor - ship,
Yon - der shines the   in - fant Light: Come and wor - ship,
Ye   have seen His   na - tal   star: Come and wor - ship,
In   His tem - ple shall ap - pear: Come and wor - ship,

come and wor - ship, Wor - ship Christ, the   new - born King!
come and wor - ship, Wor - ship Christ, the   new - born King!
come and wor - ship, Wor - ship Christ, the   new - born King!
come and wor - ship, Wor - ship Christ, the   new - born King! A - MEN.

EXERCISE 18.

God of Our Fathers, Whose Almighty Hand

NATIONAL HYMN. 10. 10. 10. 10.

DANIEL C. ROBERTS, 1841-1907   GEORGE W. WARREN, 1828-1902

Trumpets before each stanza.

1. God of our fa-thers, whose al-might-y
2. Thy love di-vine hath led us in the
3. From war's a-larms, from dead-ly pes-ti-
4. Re-fresh Thy peo-ple on their toil-some

hand   Leads forth in beau-ty all the star-ry band
past,   In this free land by Thee our lot is cast;
lence,   Be Thy strong arm our ev-er sure de-fense;
way,   Lead us from night to nev-er-end-ing day;

Of shin-ing worlds in splen-dor through the skies,
Be Thou our rul-er, guard-ian, guide, and stay,
Thy true re-li-gion in our hearts in-crease,
Fill all our lives with love and grace di-vine,

Our grate-ful songs be-fore Thy throne a-rise.
Thy Word our law, Thy paths our cho-sen way.
Thy boun-teous good-ness nour-ish us in peace.
And glo-ry, laud, and praise be ev-er Thine. A-MEN.

3. *The Expression Hand*

We have been using the expression hand thus far to indicate dynamic levels in the volume and to help in the expression of the song. It can also be used for other purposes.

It is acceptable to use the expression hand, at times, along with the lead hand to beat out the rhythm. Particularly is this true when a leader is directing a large congregation. People on all sides of the leader, to his right and to his left, in the front, and to the rear can see his beats and gestures. In beating a rhythm pattern, the expression hand performs exactly the same pattern as the lead hand except that it is reversed. For example, in 4/4 measure, the lead hand directs *down,* left, *right,* up; the expression hand moves oppositely by going *down,* right, *left,* up. The expression hand and the lead hand are thus synchronized and perfectly co-ordinated.

Except in directing large congregations, the expression hand should be used sparingly to conduct rhythm patterns. Its importance actually is related to other things. It can:

(1) Give accent or emphasis to a beat or beats.

(2) Assist the lead hand in marking the rhythm.

(3) Be used to cue in singers.

(4) Help to sustain notes, execute holds, build climaxes, and indicate tempo changes.

(5) Control dynamics and interpretive gestures.

In performing these functions the expression hand often acts independently of the lead hand and yet it is perfectly poised and synchronized in its movements as related to the work of the lead hand.

As we progress now from song to song, there will be opportunities for the director to use his expression hand much more effectively than heretofore.

The leader should practice diligently on the various uses of the expression hand in order to make his leading much more effective. All music should be beautifully expressed through the finest interpretation it is possible for the director to achieve. This calls for effective use of arms, hands, eyes, face, and body movements. The better a director can use these physical assets to interpret the music, the more effective will be his ministry.

"There Is Power in the Blood"

For many years we have sung this gospel hymn and we enjoy using it in revivals and informal services. It has an exceptionally fine flow of 4/4 rhythm and should be directed with precise beats. The stanzas should be directed with accents on 1 and 3 because of the importance of the words. In the refrain, the expression hand may serve to hold the half notes and dotted half notes of the soprano and alto parts while the lead hand beats the rhythm of the tenor and bass. Practice using the expression hand in this manner, holding it up to sustain the words which are held while the men's voices are moving. Repeat several times.

EXERCISE 19.

There Is Power in the Blood

POWER IN THE BLOOD. 10. 9. 10. 8. with Refrain

Lewis E. Jones, 1865-1936   Lewis E. Jones, 1865-1936

1. Would you be free from the bur - den of sin? There's pow'r in the blood,
2. Would you be free from your pas - sion and pride? There's pow'r in the blood,
3. Would you be whit - er, much whit - er than snow? There's pow'r in the blood,
4. Would you do serv - ice for Je - sus your King? There's pow'r in the blood,

pow'r in the blood; Would you o'er e - vil a vic - to - ry win? There's
pow'r in the blood; Come for a cleans - ing to Cal - va - ry's tide; There's
pow'r in the blood; Sin stains are lost in its life - giv - ing flow; There's
pow'r in the blood; Would you live dai - ly His prais - es to sing? There's

Refrain

won - der - ful pow'r in the blood. There is pow'r, pow'r, Wonder-working pow'r
there is

In the blood of the Lamb; There is pow'r, pow'r,
In the blood of the Lamb; there is

Won - der - work - ing pow'r In the pre - cious blood of the Lamb.

"Rejoice, Ye Pure in Heart"

Make much of the word "rejoice" in this song. From the very beginning it should be emphasized. The refrain can be made thrilling by a skilful use of the "rejoices."

For a different approach, suppose we use *both* the hands all the way through this song, but use the expression hand in a dual role to mark rhythm and sustain notes. For the preparatory beat, raise the lead hand to the "attention" position and raise the expression hand to a like position on the left. As the preparatory beat is executed, bring both hands inward and upward, describing the arc necessary for completing the preparatory beat and following through with the

EXERCISE 20.

Rejoice, Ye Pure in Heart

MARION. S. M. with Refrain

EDWARD H. PLUMPTRE, 1821-1891

ARTHUR H. MESSITER, 1834-1916

1. Re - joice, ye pure in heart, Re - joice, give thanks and sing;
2. Bright youth and snow-crowned age, Strong men and maid - ens fair,
3. Yes, on through life's long path, Still chant - ing as ye go;
4. Still lift your stand - ard high, Still march in firm ar - ray,

Your glo - rious ban - ner wave on high, The cross of Christ your King.
Raise high your free, ex - ult - ing song, God's won-drous praise de - clare.
From youth to age, by night and day, In glad - ness and in woe.
As war - riors thro' the dark - ness toil Till dawns the gold - en day.

REFRAIN

Re - joice, re - joice, Re - joice, give thanks and sing. A-MEN.
Re - joice, re - joice,

59

EXERCISE 21.

There's a Glad New Song

REDEEMING LOVE.   10. 8. 10. 8.   with Refrain

ALBERT C. FISHER, 1886-1946

ALBERT C. FISHER, 1886-1946

1. There's a glad new song ring-ing in my heart, Such as an-gels would
2. When my soul was lost in a star-less night Where my feet nev-er
3. When at last I stand with the heav-'nly choir In the light of the

sing a-bove, And the whole day long it doth joy im-part;
ceased to rove, At a dread-ful cost Je-sus brought me light,
throne a-bove, On the gold-en strand I shall nev-er tire

REFRAIN

'Tis the song of re-deem-ing love.
All be-cause of re-deem-ing love. Of His love...... I shall
Of the song of re-deem-ing love. Of His love

ev-er sing Till a-bove...... I be-hold the King; Through e-
Till a-bove

ter-ni-ty my glad song shall be Of the Sav-iour's re-deem-ing love.

downbeat 1. Both hands come down simultaneously and beat out the first measure, working in exact but opposite patterns. In M.2, hold the expression hand up for three counts on the word "heart" while the lead hand beats out the rhythm. Now bring the expression hand back into synchronization with the lead hand on count 4 and conduct M.3 with both hands. Treat M.4 the same as M.2, then conduct M.5-6-7 with both hands and M.8 with the expression hand sustaining the note as the lead hand beats time. On the refrain, use the expression hand to sustain the dotted half notes of "rejoice" while the lead hand indicates the rhythm for the men's voices. Close the refrain by using both hands on next to the last measure and by sustaining the last note with both hands extended in a *hold* position. Release with a cutoff after three counts by bringing both hands in and down sharply in a cutoff stroke.

Synchronizing the use of both hands may present a few problems at first, but practice the song many times until you master this technique. It may be necessary to learn to control each hand separately and then use them together.

"There's a Glad New Song"

Some of the techniques of the expression hand used in the two previous songs may be utilized in "There's a Glad New Song." Observe that it begins on an upbeat; therefore, the preparatory beat goes out before cuing in the singers on 4. The refrain has sustained notes to be held by the expression hand as the lead hand beats out the other parts.

II. Modified Diagram for Four-Beat Measure

Just as we use modified beats in duple (two-beat) and triple (three-beat) measure, even so do we use them in quadruple (four-beat) measure. The nature of the song determines how angular or flowing the pattern should be. Some songs are slower and more free flowing than others and consequently call for a rounded flowing beat. *Direction,* however, remains the same. The modified four-beat diagram would appear similar to Illustration 26.

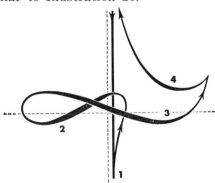

Illus. 26. Modified Four-Beat Measure

It Is Well with My Soul

VILLE DE HAVRE. **11. 8. 11. 9. with Refrain**

HORATIO G. SPAFFORD, 1828-1888   PHILIP P. BLISS 1838-1876

1. When peace, like a riv-er, at-tend-eth my way, When sor-rows like
2. Though Sa-tan should buf-fet, tho' tri-als should come, Let this blest as-
3. My sin— oh, the bliss of this glo-ri-ous tho't: My sin not in
4. And, Lord, haste the day when the faith shall be sight, The clouds be roll'd

sea bil-lows roll; What-ev-er my lot, Thou hast taught me to say,
sur-ance con-trol, That Christ has re-gard-ed my help-less es-tate,
part, but the whole Is nail'd to the cross and I bear it no more,
back as a scroll, The trump shall re-sound and the Lord shall de-scend,

REFRAIN

It is well, it is well with my soul.
And hath shed his own blood for my soul.
Praise the Lord, praise the Lord, O my soul!
"E-ven so," it is well with my soul.

It is well   with my

It is well

soul,   It is well, it is well with my soul.
with my soul,

"It Is Well with My Soul"

This hymn offers tremendous possibility for dynamic contrast. Use both hands for effective interpretation. The expression hand will indicate dynamic levels through the stanzas and synchronize with the lead hand in the refrain by holding the soprano line as the right hand beats the rhythm and indicates entrance of the voice parts. Work for smoothness by using the beat of Illustration 26.

Songs in 4/2 Measure

We beat 4/2 measure the same as 4/4. There is no difference. Often a 4/2 song will be slower than one in 4/4, but the time signature is not always the determining factor. The type of song, its construction, message, and rhythmic structure all join to determine the tempo.

In 4/2 measure we present two songs. The first is a minor tune setting of "Jesus, Lover of My Soul." The second is "O Sacred Head Now Wounded."

"Jesus, Lover of My Soul" ("Aberystwyth") (Ex. 23)

This setting of a universally loved hymn has unusual appeal. The key is minor and the parts are effectively treated. Study the hymn first for its message, then its structure. Observe the moving parts and the opportunities for expression. The first measure is full; therefore, we begin with a downbeat.

"O Sacred Head, Now Wounded" (Ex. 24)

We now conduct a hymn which is quite different in nature from some of the others we have been directing. It is a "passion chorale" expressing the passion of our Lord. It must be directed with a sympathetic, even flow which expresses the mood of the song. Use both hands to fully express the dramatic content and intensity of the message.

FOR FURTHER STUDY

Practice the following quadruple-measure hymns:

Christ, Whose Glory Fills the Skies

Awake, My Soul, in Joyful Lays

Guide Me, O Thou Great Jehovah (Cwm Rhondda)

Come, Ye Faithful, Raise the Strain

Crown Him with Many Crowns

EXERCISE 23.

Jesus, Lover of My Soul

ABERYSTWYTH. 7. 7. 7. 7. D.

CHARLES WESLEY, 1707-1788

JOSEPH PARRY, 1841-1903

1. Je - sus, lov - er of my soul, Let me to Thy bos - om fly,
2. Oth - er ref - uge have I none; Hangs my help - less soul on Thee;
3. Thou, O Christ, art all I want; More than all in Thee I find;
4. Plen - teous grace with Thee is found, Grace to cov - er all my sin;

While the near - er wa - ters roll, While the tem - pest still is high:
Leave, O leave me not a - lone, Still sup - port and com - fort me:
Raise the fall - en, cheer the faint, Heal the sick, and lead the blind:
Let the heal - ing streams a - bound; Make and keep me pure with - in:

Hide me, O my Sav - iour, hide, Till the storm of life is past;
All my trust on Thee is stayed, All my help from Thee I bring;
Just and ho - ly is Thy name, I am all un - right - eous - ness;
Thou of life the foun - tain art, Free - ly let me take of Thee;

Safe in - to the ha - ven guide; O re - ceive my soul at last.
Cov - er my de - fense-less head With the shad - ow of Thy wing.
False and full of sin I am, Thou art full of truth and grace.
Spring Thou up with - in my heart, Rise to all e - ter - ni - ty. A - MEN.

Tune used by permission of Hughes and Sons, 16 Westgate Street, Cardiff

O Sacred Head, Now Wounded

PASSION CHORALE. 7. 6. 7. 6. D.

Authorship Uncertain
Tr. by PAUL GERHARDT, 1607-1676
Tr. by JAMES W. ALEXANDER, 1804-1859

HANS L. HASSLER, 1564-1612
Harmonized by J. S. BACH, 1685-1750

1. O sa - cred Head, now wound-ed, With grief and shame weighed down,
2. What Thou, my Lord, hast suf - fered Was all for sin - ners' gain:
3. What lan - guage shall I bor - row To thank Thee, dear- est Friend,

Now scorn-ful - ly sur - round -ed With thorns, Thine on - ly crown;
Mine, mine was the trans - gres -sion, But Thine the dead - ly pain;
For this Thy dy - ing sor - row, Thy pit - y with - out end?

How pale Thou art with an - guish, With sore a - buse and scorn!
Lo, here I fall, my Sav - iour! 'Tis I de - serve Thy place;
O make me Thine for - ev - er, And should I faint - ing be,

How does that vis - age lan - guish Which once was bright as morn!
Look on me with Thy fa - vor, Vouch-safe to me Thy grace.
Lord, let me nev - er, nev - er Out - live my love to Thee. A - MEN.

CHAPTER 6 OUTLINE

6
Six-Beat Measure

I. Six Beats to the Measure

A measure of six beats is equal to two measures of three beats each. In three-beat measure the accent is on beat 1. Thus, a measure of sextuple time would have accents on beat 1 and beat 4. The accent on 4, however, is called a secondary accent because it is subordinate to beat 1 of the measure, which *always* receives the primary accent in any measure. There are times when the secondary accent needs to be as strong as the primary accent in order to give emphasis to a word or create a special effect. Generally speaking, however, the secondary accent receives less weight in conducting. In counting a six-beat measure, we speak, *1*, 2, 3, *4*, 5, 6. By emphasizing 1 and 4 as we speak the six-beat measure a number of times, we begin to feel the symmetry and flow of sextuple measure.

1. *Explanation of Diagram*

There are numerous methods in use today for beating six-beat measure. The one in most common use is the old German style beat of DOWN, in, in, OUT, up, up. In using this style, the secondary accent on 4 has better opportunity for accented expression because the hand is going out from the body on a rather long stroke that corresponds somewhat, except for direction, to the long downstroke used on the primary accent of 1. A simple diagram of six-beat measure is rather difficult to illustrate, but the *direction* is something like this:

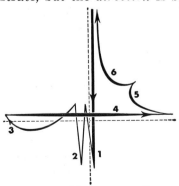

Illus. 27. Six-Beat Measure—German Style

Fast coming into popular use is the Italian style beat, which takes a general form of the duple beat and lends itself to an easy transition from beating a six-beat measure to a measure with beats only on the accents. The Italian style beat may be used with facility in a song which must be conducted with six beats, but which moves in a faster tempo than some of the slow sextuple hymns. The diagram looks something like this:

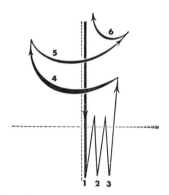

Illus. 28. SIX-BEAT MEASURE—ITALIAN STYLE

For our purpose in general song leading, perhaps it is better that we use the German style (Illus. 27). However, the student will surely wish to get the feel of both beats even though he will probably utilize the German style for his leading of songs. The illustrations given (27 and 28) show the simple six-beat pattern. For the modified form, the beats will be rounded off as in preceding patterns, while the direction of each beat is preserved.

2. *Songs in Six-Beat Measure*

Practice the six-beat diagram (Illus. 27) a number of times, counting *1*, 2, 3, *4,* 5, 6; *1*, 2, 3, *4,* 5, 6, etc.

"Breathe on Me"

This is one of the late B. B. McKinney's best songs. It is devotional and prayerful in content, and should be directed with earnestness and sustained phrasing. It has great potential for expressiveness through dynamic contrast and the moving voice parts.

Study the song carefully and direct it with six beats to the measure. Be careful not to set a tempo so slow that it will kill the effectiveness, nor so fast that it will conceal the message. Phrase it carefully.

68

Breathe on Me

TRUETT. 7. 6. 8. 6. with Refrain

Edwin Hatch, 1835-1889
Alt. by B. B. McKinney, 1886-1952

B. B. McKinney, 1886-1952

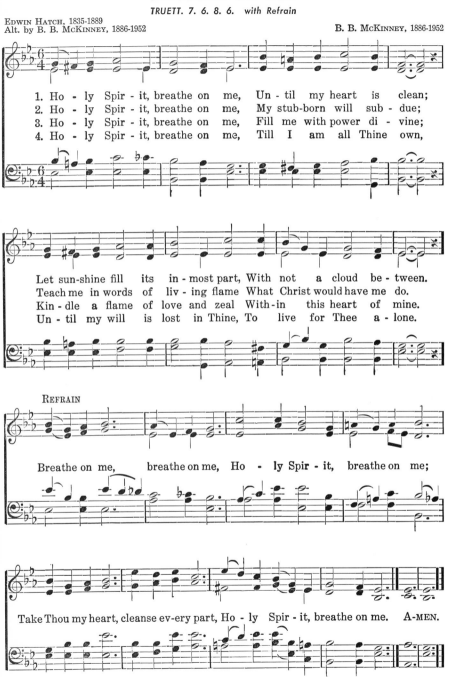

1. Ho - ly Spir - it, breathe on me, Un - til my heart is clean;
2. Ho - ly Spir - it, breathe on me, My stub-born will sub - due;
3. Ho - ly Spir - it, breathe on me, Fill me with power di - vine;
4. Ho - ly Spir - it, breathe on me, Till I am all Thine own,

Let sun-shine fill its in - most part, With not a cloud be - tween.
Teach me in words of liv - ing flame What Christ would have me do.
Kin - dle a flame of love and zeal With - in this heart of mine.
Un - til my will is lost in Thine, To live for Thee a - lone.

Refrain

Breathe on me, breathe on me, Ho - ly Spir - it, breathe on me;

Take Thou my heart, cleanse ev-ery part, Ho - ly Spir - it, breathe on me. A-men.

© Copyright 1937 by The Sunday School Board of the Southern Baptist Convention

"Seal Us, O Holy Spirit"

The rhythm of this song is marked 6/8. It should be directed slightly faster than "Breathe on Me," and the beats should be a bit more crisp.

"My Soul in Sad Exile" (Ex. 27)

Begin this song on an upbeat. A preparatory beat will first be given and the singers will be brought in as the hand gestures to them and sweeps up on count 6. Beat the 6/4 rhythm in a steady manner, accenting counts 1 and 4 of each measure.

II. TWO-BEAT COMPOUND MEASURE

1. *Explanation of Diagram*

Many songs in sextuple measure should be sung at a rather fast tempo which makes it very impractical to try to beat them in six beats. To solve this situation, we use what we call the compound duple beat. Remembering that six-beat measure has accents on 1 and 4, we simply beat out the accented beats. This means that we use a two-beat pattern, the first three beats of the 6 counts being in 1 and the last three beats being in 2. The hand would beat time down and up and we would count *1*, 2, 3, on the downstroke and *4*, 5, 6, on the upstroke. The diagram of compound duple measure would take this shape:

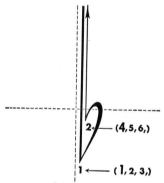

Illus. 29. COMPOUND DUPLE MEASURE

2. *Songs in Compond Duple Measure*

"Lord, Send a Revival" (Ex. 28)

This revival song is written in 6/4 measure, but should be conducted in two beats to each measure. It divides very naturally into a duple beat. Notice the first measure. The first three quarter notes are sung on the *down*beat and the next three on the *up*beat. Both beats are accented—the first as the hand strikes the bottom of the downstroke and the second as the rebound strikes 2.

70

Seal Us, O Holy Spirit

CARSON. 7. 7. 8. 7. with Refrain

Isaac H. Meredith, 1872-

Isaac H. Meredith, 1872-

1. Seal us, O Ho - ly Spir - it, Grant us Thine im-press, we pray;
2. Seal us, O Ho - ly Spir - it, Help us Thy like-ness to show;
3. Seal us, O Ho - ly Spir - it, Make us Thine own from this hour;

We would be more like the Sav-iour, Stamped with His im-age to - day.
Then from our life un - to oth - ers Streams of rich bless-ings shall flow.
Let us be use - ful, dear Mas - ter, Seal us with wit-ness-ing power.

Refrain

Seal us, seal us, Seal us just now, we pray; Seal us, O

Ho - ly Spir - it, Seal us for serv - ice to - day. A - men.

My Soul in Sad Exile

HAVEN OF REST. Irregular with Refrain

HENRY L. GILMOUR, 1837-1920

GEORGE D. MOORE

1. My soul in sad ex - ile was out on life's sea, So bur-dened with
2. I yield - ed my - self to His ten - der em-brace, And faith tak - ing
3. The song of my soul, since the Lord made me whole, Has been the old
4. Oh, come to the Sav - iour, He pa - tient-ly waits To save by His

sin and dis - trest, Till I heard a sweet voice say-ing "Make Me your choice,"
hold of the word, My fet-ters fell off, and I an - chored my soul:
sto - ry so blest, Of Je - sus who'll save who-so - ev - er will have
pow - er di - vine; Come, an - chor your soul in the ha - ven of rest,

REFRAIN

And I en-tered the ha - ven of rest.
The ha - ven of rest is my Lord.
A home in the ha - ven of rest. I've an-chored my soul in the
And say, "My Be - lov - ed is mine."

ha - ven of rest, I'll sail the wide seas no more; The tem - pest may

sweep o'er the wild storm-y deep, In Je - sus I'm safe ev - er - more.

EXERCISE 28.

Lord, Send a Revival

MATTHEWS. 9. 9. 9. 7. with Refrain

B. B. McKinney, 1886-1952   B. B. McKinney, 1886-1952

1. Send a re-viv-al, O Christ, my Lord, Let it go o-ver the land and sea,
2. Send a re-viv-al a-mong Thine own, Help us to turn from our sins a-way,
3. Send a re-viv-al to those in sin, Help them, O Je-sus, to turn to Thee,
4. Send a re-viv-al in ev-'ry heart, Draw the world nearer, O Lord, to Thee,

Send it ac-cord-ing to Thy dear Word, And let it be-gin in me.
Let us get near-er the Father's throne, Re-vive us a-gain, we pray.
Let them the new life in Thee be-gin, Oh, give them the vic-to-ry.
Let Thy sal-va-tion true joy im-part, And let it be-gin in me.

REFRAIN

Lord, send a re-viv-al, Lord, send a re-viv-al,

Lord, send a re-viv-al, And let it be-gin in me.

By using the regular preparatory beat for beginning on a downbeat, and by using a steady two-beat pattern throughout the entire song, the director should be able to conduct with precision and clarity and produce good results.

"There Is a Name I Love to Hear"

Written in 6/8 time, this song naturally divides itself into a two-beat measure. Study the groupings of the notes, particularly in the refrain. A dotted quarter note becomes the basic beat note. Actually it is possible to express a time such as this by using a time signature of the figure 2 over a dotted quarter note. We recognize, of course, that a dotted quarter note equals a quarter note plus an eighth note, or three eighth notes.

Since the song begins on a pickup note, we use the preparatory beat such as is presented in Illustration 20. Conduct the song with an even and smooth-flowing beat, and give emphasis to the first beat in each measure of the refrain.

"Sweet Peace, the Gift of God's Love" (Ex. 30)

There are several things we want to observe as we direct this song. First, we beat it in duple time. Second, we begin on a pickup similar to Exercise 29. Third, at the beginning of the second measure we sustain the tied notes with the expression hand as we beat the rhythm for the altos and tenors. This is repeated on the next two measures. Fourth, we use expressive beats on the refrain, interpreting the word "peace" somewhat quietly, then emphasizing the word "wonderful." Fifth, we build a nice climax in the last score. This song can be very effectively interpreted, and we suggest the leader study it carefully to develop its meaning and message to the fullest.

There Is a Name I Love to Hear

OH, HOW I LOVE JESUS. **C. M. with Refrain**

FREDERICK WHITFIELD, 1829-1904

Anonymous

1. There is a name I love to hear, I love to sing its worth;
2. It tells me of a Sav-iour's love, Who died to set me free;
3. It tells me what my Fa-ther hath In store for ev - 'ry day,
4. It tells of One whose lov-ing heart Can feel my deep-est woe,

It sounds like mu - sic in mine ear, The sweet-est name on earth.
It tells me of His pre - cious blood, The sin - ner's per - fect plea.
And though I tread a dark-some path, Yields sun-shine all the way.
Who in each sor - row bears a part, That none can bear be - low.

REFRAIN

Oh, how I love Je - sus, Oh, how I love Je - sus,

Oh, how I love Je - sus, Be - cause He first loved me.

EXERCISE 30.

Sweet Peace, the Gift of God's Love

SWEET PEACE. L. M. with Refrain

PETER P. BILHORN, 1861-1936

PETER P. BILHORN, 1861-1936

1. There comes to my heart one sweet strain (sweet strain), A glad and a joy-ous re-frain (re-frain); I sing it a-gain and a-gain, Sweet peace, the gift of God's love.

2. Through Christ on the cross peace was made (was made), My debt by His death was all paid (all paid); No oth-er foun-da-tion is laid For peace, the gift of God's love.

3. In Je-sus for peace I a-bide (a-bide), And as I keep close to His side (His side), There's noth-ing but peace doth be-tide, Sweet peace, the gift of God's love.

REFRAIN

Peace, peace, sweet peace! Won-der-ful gift from a-bove (a-bove)! Oh, won-der-ful, won-der-ful peace! Sweet peace, the gift of God's love!

FOR FURTHER STUDY

Practice the following sextuple-measure hymns:

The Old Rugged Cross

All Things Bright and Beautiful

Day Is Dying in the West

It Came upon the Midnight Clear

There Is a Green Hill Far Away

CHAPTER 7 OUTLINE

  I. NINE-BEAT MEASURE

      1. Explanation of Diagram

      2. Compound Triple Pattern

      3. Songs in Compound Triple Measure

  II. TWELVE-BEAT MEASURE

      1. Explanation of Diagram

      2. Compound Quadruple Pattern

      3. Compound Quadruple Song

7

Multiple Beat Measures

I. NINE-BEAT MEASURE

Few, if any, hymns are sung nine beats to the measure. Some choral and instrumental music is written to be so conducted, but the song leader will rarely come in contact with a nine-beat measure. The measure is written as 9/8 or 9/4.

1. *Explanation of Diagram*

Although it is unlikely that the song leader will need to conduct music in nine-beat measure, it is important that he master the nine-beat pattern. Learning its direction and flow will greatly assist him later in using subdivided beats of triple time. Actually, a nine-beat pattern takes somewhat the general shape of a three-beat pattern. We understand why this is true when we realize that a nine-beat pattern is made up of *three* three-beat measures and that it is usually conducted as a triple-measure pattern. Therefore, accents occur on counts 1, 4, and 7. Nine-beat measure is counted *1*, 2, 3, *4*, 5, 6, *7*, 8, 9, etc. The diagram takes this shape:

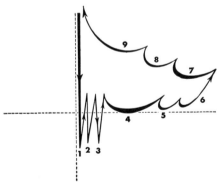

Illus. 30. NINE-BEAT MEASURE

2. *Compound Triple Pattern*

In actual practice, the song leader will treat 9/8 and 9/4 songs as if they were written in triple measure. The figure 9/8 could be written as a 3 over a dotted quarter note. We reduce 9/8 measure to three beats

79

to the measure and use a dotted quarter (equal to a quarter note plus an eighth note or three eighth notes) as the basic beat (♩. = ♪♪♪ or ♩ ♪). Or in 9/4 measure, we use three beats, and the basic beat is a dotted half note (♩. = ♩♩♩ or ♩ ♩). We use the same three-beat diagrams as presented in chapter 4.

In drawing the pattern of compound triple measure, we use the same pattern as in Illustration 23 with accents on each of the three counts. The diagram is:

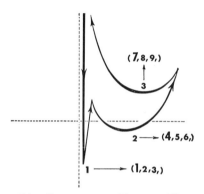

Illus. 31. COMPOUND TRIPLE MEASURE

3. Songs in Compound Triple Measure

"Blessed Assurance, Jesus Is Mine"

One of the best known of the 9/8 gospel songs is Fanny Crosby's "Blessed Assurance, Jesus Is Mine." The leader will readily see how the song is divided into dotted quarter notes and their equivalents. It is conducted, therefore, in three beats to each measure. Illustration 31 is the beat pattern which begins on an upbeat. To get the singers started, a clear preparatory beat outward is given before gesturing the first word on the upbeat. The first three notes actually could be mentally counted, 7, 8, 9, during the upbeat.

"Free from the Law, O Happy Condition" (Ex. 32)

The construction of this song is almost identical with "Blessed Assurance," but because it is not so well known, study should be expended in learning to conduct it.

"While We Pray and While We Plead" (Ex. 33)

This song, also in 9/8 measure, begins on an upbeat. Particular attention should be given to bringing in the men's voices at various times in the refrain. Conduct the entire song with a smooth-flowing beat in order to bring out the message more effectively.

Blessed Assurance, Jesus Is Mine

ASSURANCE. 9. 10. 9. 9. with Refrain

FANNY J. CROSBY, 1820-1915　　　　　　　　　　MRS. JOSEPH F. KNAPP, 1839-1908

1. Bless - ed as - sur - ance, Je - sus is mine! Oh, what a fore - taste of
2. Per - fect sub - mis - sion, per - fect de - light, Vi - sions of rap - ture now
3. Per - fect sub - mis - sion, all is at rest, I in my Sav - iour am

glo - ry di - vine! Heir of sal - va - tion, pur-chase of God,
burst on my sight: An - gels de - scend - ing bring from a - bove
hap - py and blest: Watch-ing and wait - ing, look - ing a - bove,

REFRAIN

Born of His Spir - it, wash'd in His blood.
Ech - oes of mer - cy, whis-pers of love.　This is my sto - ry, this is my
Fill'd with His good-ness, lost in His love.

song, Prais-ing my Sav - iour all the day long; This is my sto - ry,

this is my song, Prais-ing my Sav - iour all the day long.

EXERCISE 32.

Free from the Law, O Happy Condition

ONCE FOR ALL. 10. 10. 9. 8. with Refrain

PHILIP P. BLISS, 1838-1876

PHILIP P. BLISS, 1838-1876

1. Free from the law, O hap-py con-di-tion, Je-sus hath
2. Now are we free—there's no con-dem-na-tion, Je-sus pro-
3. "Chil-dren of God," O glo-ri-ous call-ing, Sure-ly His

bled, and there is re-mis-sion; Cursed by the law and bruised by the
vides a per-fect sal-va-tion; "Come un-to Me," O hear His sweet
grace will keep us from fall-ing; Pass-ing from death to life at His

REFRAIN

fall, Grace hath re-deemed us once for all.
call, Come, and He saves us once for all. Once for all, O sin-ner, recall, Bless-ed sal-va-tion once for all.

ceive it, Once for all, O broth-er, be-lieve it; Cling to the

cross, the bur-den will fall, Christ hath re-deemed us once for all.

EXERCISE 33.

While We Pray and While We Plead

WHY NOT NOW? *7. 7. 7. 7. with Refrain*

Daniel W. Whittle, 1840-1901

Charles C. Case, 1843-1918

1. While we pray and while we plead, While you see your soul's deep need,
2. You have wan-dered far a - way; Do not risk an - oth - er day;
3. In the world you've failed to find Aught of peace for trou-bled mind;
4. Come to Christ, con - fes - sion make; Come to Christ, and par - don take;

While our Fa - ther calls you home, Will you not, my broth - er, come?
Do not turn from God your face, But to - day ac - cept His grace.
Come to Christ, on Him be - lieve, Peace and joy you shall re - ceive.
Trust in Him from day to day, He will keep you all the way.

REFRAIN

Why not now?.... Why not now?.... Why not come to Je - sus now?
Why not now? Why not now?

Why not now?.... Why not now?.... Why not come to Je - sus now?
Why not now? Why not now?

II. Twelve-Beat Measure

1. *Explanation of Diagram*

Although there are few hymns in which the song leader will use nine beats to the measure, there are even fewer in twelve-beat measure. Always in conducting hymns, the twelve-beat measure is reduced to compound quadruple—four beats to the measure. It is important, however, that the song leader know the twelve-beat pattern so that he will be able to subdivide beats later on in music calling for subdivided beats. The diagram for a twelve-beat measure follows that of a four-beat measure. This is true simply because most of the time the twelve-beat measure is conducted as a four-beat measure. Twelve-beat measure is counted *1*, 2, 3, *4*, 5, 6, *7*, 8, 9, *10*, 11, 12. Accents come on 1, 4, 7, and 10.

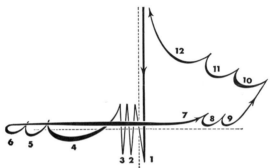

Illus. 32. Twelve-Beat Measure

2. *Compound Quadruple Pattern*

The twelve-beat pattern in Illustration 32 follows the contour of a regular four-beat pattern such as was presented in chapter 5. All hymns written in 12/8 and 12/4 measure will be reduced to four beats to each measure with the basic beat becoming either a dotted quarter note in 12/8 measure or a dotted half in 12/4 measure. Thus each count would be slightly accented since the four-beat pattern is actually a reduction of the twelve-beat pattern. The diagram of compound quadruple is:

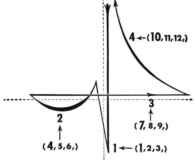

Illus. 33. Compound Quadruple Measure

3. *Compound Quadruple Song*

"More Holiness Give Me" (Ex. 34)

Observe that the song has a 12/8 signature. Also, notice how it naturally divides its notation and measures so that a dotted quarter note becomes the basic beat. The 12/8 signature would simply be translated into the figure 4 over a dotted quarter note.

This song should be conducted smoothly in four beats to the measure. After conducting it several times, try beating out, in the rhythm of one beat, the three eighth notes in each measure. Thus, you would beat three short strokes inward after your long downstroke. Then you would have a stroke outward and another one up.

More Holiness Give Me

MY PRAYER. 6. 5. 6. 5. D.

PHILIP P. BLISS, 1838-1876   PHILIP P. BLISS, 1838-1876

1. More ho - li - ness give me, More striv - ing with - in;
2. More grat - i - tude give me, More trust in the Lord;
3. More pu - ri - ty give me, More strength to o'er - come;

More pa - tience in suf - fering, More sor - row for sin;
More pride in His glo - ry, More hope in His Word;
More free - dom from earth - stains, More long - ings for home;

More faith in my Sav - iour, More sense of His care;
More tears for His sor - rows, More pain at His grief;
More fit for the king - dom, More used would I be;

More joy in His serv - ice, More pur - pose in prayer.
More meek - ness in tri - al, More praise for re - lief.
More bless - ed and ho - ly, More, Sav - iour, like Thee.   A - MEN.

FOR FURTHER STUDY

Practice the following compound-measure hymns:

One Day

Blessed Redeemer

Just When I Need Him Most

Teach Me to Pray

Have Thine Own Way, Lord

CHAPTER 8 OUTLINE

    I. CONDUCTING RHYTHM

        1. Following the Words

        2. Subdividing Beats

        3. Make Gestures Meaningful

    II. INTERPRETATION

        1. Music Flow

        2. Conducting Music, Not Notes

        3. Some Factors to Keep in Mind

    III. SONGS FOR SPECIAL INTERPRETATION

    IV. PHYSICAL SURROUNDINGS

        1. Lighting, Temperature, and Ventilation

        2. Hymnals and Instruments

        3. Materials and Copyright

        4. Correct Practice Makes Perfect

8
Making Measure Meaningful

I. CONDUCTING RHYTHM

In all of our discussion thus far we have adhered strictly to the patterns of the various duple, triple, quadruple, and compound rhythms. We have learned a definite pattern for each and that the strokes used are constant as to direction and accent. For example, in any measure the first beat is *always* down and accented. The last beat is *always* up and unaccented. Other beats and accents fall into their assigned patterns, never deviating to a great extent from that established movement.

It is possible, however, to leave out one of the beats after the rhythm is established in a song if the time of the beat is absorbed in some manner that will not create an interruption in the even flow of the rhythm or an awkwardness in the measure. It is likewise possible to divide a beat into smaller segments in order to interpret the song more effectively. Whether beats are left out or divided into segments, the general shape of the rhythm pattern must be maintained.

1. *Following the Words*

In directing a song it is good practice to try to have the hands "sing the words" in so far as is possible. We try to conduct in such a way that all movements of the hands and body are in the mood and spirit of the song. The hands say what the words express. If the words and music are crisp and joyous, the hands and manner of conducting convey that mood. If the words and music are devotional and prayerful, the conducting will be easy flowing and beautifully contoured.

In following the words we try to make our leading as clear and as easy as possible. Thus, at the end of a phrase, there may occur a note which has the value of several beats. Instead of beating this note out, it is quite acceptable to let the lead hand go down on the beat and then curve outward and upward, sustaining the note in its full value. Or, after a song is flowing, it is permissible to beat the particular words in a measure while we make sure we maintain the proper beat direction.

As an example, suppose we have this rhythm in a song which employs the down, in, out, up pattern:

$\frac{4}{4}$

Be - neath the cross of Je - sus I fain would take my stand,
Up - down - in · out · up down - out · up - down - in · out · up · down-

Obviously, we begin on an upbeat and beat four beats in the first measure. On the second measure we could use one long downbeat on the syllable "Je-" which would be the value of two counts and then an outstroke and an upstroke. This would be followed by four regular beats and the last measure would, on the word "stand," be a long downstroke, curving outward to a release after beat 3. A procedure such as beating the words would be used *only* when the expression, smoothness and meaningfulness of the song would be improved. A careful study, particularly of songs of a slow tempo and devotional nature, will reveal the passages where a minimum of conducting beats and the use of "word beats" will be most appropriate.

2. Subdividing Beats

In songs that move slowly it is often advisable to subdivide the beats. This is always done within the framework of the beat pattern. Subdividing a beat simply produces two strokes (or more) in the direction of the beat.

For example, the basic beat of "Jesus Shall Reign" is 2/2. The pattern for 2/2 is down, up. Each half note receives its regular beat, but we can subdivide the beats in which quarter notes appear. We keep the beat pattern and direction but subdivide the beat while maintaining the direction. The rhythm follows the words simply to add to the clarity and emphasis. Thus the various measure rhythms could be directed:

♩ ♩ down, up (regular beat pattern)

♩ ♩ ♩ down, up, up (two upstrokes in one beat)

𝅗𝅥 down, out (curve stroke outward with quick release stroke to position for downbeat)

♩ ♩ ♩ ♩ down, down, up, up (two down on the one beat; two up on the two beat)

♩. ♩ down, up (down for a beat and one-half; up on last half of 2)

Conduct the song, "Jesus Shall Reign," using the above rhythm.

EXERCISE 35.

Jesus Shall Reign Where'er the Sun

DUKE STREET. L. M.

Isaac Watts, 1674-1748

John Hatton, d. 1793

1. Je - sus shall reign wher - e'er the sun Does his suc-
2. From north to south the princ - es meet To pay their
3. To Him shall end - less pray'r be made, And end - less
4. Peo - ple and realms of ev - 'ry tongue Dwell on His

ces - sive jour - neys run; His king-dom spread from shore to shore,
hom - age at His feet; While west-ern em - pires own their Lord,
prais - es crown His head; His name like sweet per - fume shall rise
love with sweet-est song, And in - fant voic - es shall pro - claim

Till moons shall wax and wane no more.
And sav - age tribes at - tend His word.
With ev - 'ry morn - ing sac - ri - fice.
Their ear - ly bless - ings on His name. A - MEN.

3. Make Gestures Meaningful

We cannot overemphasize the importance of clarity in the conducting strokes. To make the hands describe meaningless circles, flourishes, and unnecessary motions is very confusing to the singers. It is best to try to conserve distances and motion in order to make each gesture meaningful.

All attacks should be direct and clean with singers and accompanist coming in exactly on time and at the instant of the beat. Clear-cut beats should begin each phrase and each stanza. Time of one or two beats or even more should be allowed between stanzas in order to permit the

91

people to breathe and then come in together exactly on the first word. Releases are as important as attacks. The director should keep the song moving and should bring out the ends of phrases in a way that keeps the people singing until time for the cutoff. He may do so most easily by simply keeping the hands moving outward and upward until time for the release. At the end of a song the leader will sustain the last tones through the sustaining gesture of upraised and slowly-moving hands until time for the release at which time he uses a cutoff stroke. All attacks and releases should be clear and precise and definite so that no one will fail to understand.

The size of the beats should be kept in proportion to the size of the crowd. It is not necessary to have great sweeping gestures when conducting a small group of people. It is best for the director to establish the limits of the "field of beating" for each situation—a wide field for a crowd of hundreds, even thousands, of people, and a smaller field for smaller groups. Within the field which he establishes he will proportionately utilize the strokes denoting dynamic levels.

II. INTERPRETATION

1. *Music Flow*

A director who feels the music within himself and is perfectly at ease in conducting any time signature in any type of song is in a wonderful position to help people sing with spirit and understanding. His gestures, beats, and movements are so natural and so much a part of himself that the music seems to flow right through him. The people feel a desire to sing when the director conducts with ease and sincerity.

2. *Conducting Music, Not Notes*

Mastering the various techniques and letting the music flow through his personality and gestures enables a director to make his conducting look like music. Songs are made up of phrases, sentences, and thoughts. Notes, rests, and rhythm are used simply for the purpose of helping to express these thoughts. The conductor therefore wants to use everything at his command to combine notes, rests, and rhythm in such a manner as to turn out beautiful phrases and complete thoughts. He will use his technique to build phrases and connect them in a way that will develop the complete message.

In exercising his technical facility he will make full use of volume control, using large beats for loud music and small beats for soft music. He will build crescendos with beats that grow as he indicates more volume with his expression hand. From volume peaks he will make discreet use of decrescendos. For lively music he will use crisp beats; for slow music he will use sustained and smooth-flowing beats. Sometimes he will use the vigorous attack; at other times the attack will be soft. His beats will vary with each shade of meaning, and his hands will say exactly what he wishes the song to express.

3. *Some Factors to Keep in Mind*

In order for the director to conduct musically he should be as familiar as possible with the music. What are the signatures? What should be the tempo? Is there a traditional interpretation? Are there dynamic markings to be observed? What is the message of the song? Why is it to be sung on this occasion? He should ask himself all of these questions and develop a sensitivity as to the spirit and interpretation, the rise and fall of the phrases, and other elements that will help make the song more meaningful to those who sing it.

He should also study the message of the song. He will note its construction. Since most songs contain sixteen measures, and a phrase is usually four measures, he will study each phrase, combining the

EXERCISE 36.

Sun of My Soul, Thou Saviour Dear

HURSLEY. L. M.

JOHN KEBLE, 1792-1866

Adapted from *Katholisches Gesangbuch*, c. 1774

1. Sun of my soul, Thou Sav - iour dear, It is not
2. A - bide with me from morn till eve, For with - out
3. If some poor wan - d'ring child of Thine Have spurn'd to-
4. Come near and bless us when we wake, Ere thro' the

night if Thou be near; Oh, may no earth - born
Thee I can - not live; A - bide with me when
day the voice di - vine, Now, Lord, the gra - cious
world our way we take, Till in the o - cean

cloud a - rise To hide Thee from Thy serv - ant's eyes.
night is nigh, For with - out Thee I dare not die.
work be - gin; Let him no more lie down in sin.
of Thy love We lose our - selves in heav'n a - bove. A - MEN.

EXERCISE 37.

My Jesus, I Love Thee

GORDON. *11. 11. 11. 11.*

WILLIAM R. FEATHERSTONE, 1842-1878   ADONIRAM J. GORDON, 1836-1895

1. My Je - sus, I love Thee, I know Thou art mine,
2. I love Thee be - cause Thou hast first lov - ed me,
3. I'll love Thee in life, I will love Thee in death,
4. In man - sions of glo - ry and end - less de - light

For Thee all the fol - lies of sin I re - sign;
And pur - chased my par - don on Cal - va - ry's tree;
And praise Thee as long as Thou lend - est me breath;
I'll ev - er a - dore Thee in heav - en so bright;

My gra - cious Re - deem - er, my Sav - iour art Thou;
I love Thee for wear - ing the thorns on Thy brow;
And say when the death dew lies cold on my brow,
I'll sing with the glit - ter - ing crown on my brow,

If ev - er I loved Thee, my Je - sus, 'tis now.
If ev - er I loved Thee, my Je - sus, 'tis now.
If ev - er I loved Thee, my Je - sus, 'tis now.
If ev - er I loved Thee, my Je - sus, 'tis now. A-MEN.

phrases into sentences and the sentences into the message of the song. Understanding it, he will then be able to interpret each phrase in relation to the whole and to express the flow, volume, tempo, melody, and harmony essential to the most effective presentation of the song.

III. SONGS FOR SPECIAL INTERPRETATION

Having set forth suggestions concerning interpretation, we present here two familiar hymns for the student to interpret for himself. He should study the rhythmic structures, phrasing, beat patterns, possibilities for volume contrasts, and possible use of various interpretive features and relate them to the over-all message.

"Sun of My Soul, Thou Saviour Dear" (Ex. 36)

"My Jesus, I Love Thee" (Ex. 37)

IV. PHYSICAL SURROUNDINGS

1. *Lighting, Temperature, and Ventilation*

A song leader can do much to help people sing without their being aware that he is so doing. Conditions need to be as nearly perfect as possible when people are to sing. If the room or auditorium is gloomy, chilly, or hot, the people become uncomfortable and fail to respond to the song leader's directing. It will help, therefore, if someone will check the lighting and see that it is bright enough to make the surroundings cheerful. The same person may also check temperature and ventilation. If people are too hot or too cold or drowsy because of stale air, they will not sing. The prudent song leader will, therefore, check on the lighting, temperature, and ventilation and do what he can to make the people comfortable. In so doing he overcomes the physical hurdle which frequently prevents the people's singing.

2. *Hymnals and Instruments*

The proper distribution of hymnals is another factor in helping people sing. Before a service begins it is good practice to see that there are ample hymnals available and that they are evenly distributed. No effort should be spared to make it *easy* for a person to take up a hymnal and sing.

The instrument should always be kept in tune and in perfect mechanical condition. A wheezy organ or banjo-sounding piano will have a devastating effect upon the people. The instrument should be located so that the accompanist can easily see the song leader. It is impossible for an accompanist to follow a leader whom he cannot see.

3. *Materials and Copyright*

If any materials other than hymnals are to be used in the service, they should be provided far in advance of date needed. Frequently, the leader may wish to use music or words other than those in the hymnal. If material or music is produced by a publisher, it should be ordered for use. Under no circumstances should copyrighted material or music be reproduced without permission.

Any words or music protected by copyright usually carries a copyright line which includes the word "copyright" and often the symbol ©.

When you see the word "copyright" or the distinctive © printed on a piece of music, you see a two-sided signal; it is the signal that protects the creator of the work and allows him to secure the fruits of his labor, and at the same time it is the signal that informs you that the following acts, unless authorized by the copyright proprietor, will subject you to liability under the United States Copyright Law.

These acts are copyright infringements, regardless of the purpose or type of use, even when it is for education, religion, drama, or just for pleasure:

Reprinting or copying the work or any part of it by any means whatsoever.

Arranging, adapting, or orchestrating the work or any part of it.

Recording the work for any purpose by any means, without complying with legal formalities.

Photographing the work or any part of it on film or slides, or reproducing it by opaque projector.

Performing the work in public for profit.

Making, selling, or dealing in any way with these types of infringements.

To avoid infringement, the right to do each or any of these acts must be cleared, and the clearance of one particular right does not clear any of the other rights. All rights are separate, distinct, and independent. For instance, the clearance for broadcast does not carry with it the right to copy or to arrange or to record; clearance of the right to record does not carry with it the right to perform. The obligation is upon you to make certain that the right involved in the act you intend to do has been cleared.

4. *Correct Practice Makes Perfect*

Only through diligent and correct practice will a song leader become a successful one. It is suggested, therefore, that he practice the material in this book many times and that he keep his hymnal convenient for practicing the hundreds of hymns in it. The song leader should never miss an opportunity to lead people in singing. Through actually leading people to sing he will be able to use all his newly-acquired technical knowledge for the benefit of others.

FOR FURTHER STUDY

Practice the following songs, using the style of conducting the words:

> Purer in Heart, O God
> Almost Persuaded
> Break Thou the Bread of Life
> Fairest Lord Jesus
> Oh, for a Closer Walk

CHAPTER 9 OUTLINE

    I. UNUSUAL MEASURE RHYTHMS

        1. Combination of Triple and Quadruple Rhythms

        2. Combinations of Compound Measures

    II. EXTENDED SONG FORMS

9
Mixed Measure
and Extended Song Forms

I. Unusual Measure Rhythms

In this chapter we wish to present some of the unusual measure rhythms which the song leader will encounter as he leads singing in various assemblies, services, and meetings. The hymns we have studied thus far have one time signature which governs the beat pattern to be used throughout the entire song. There are selections, however, in which the composer uses two different time signatures in order to give emphasis, create special effects, and better interpret unusual metrical structures. Most frequently he does so by writing the stanza in one time signature and the refrain in another. Occasionally, he uses a double signature, such as 3/4 4/4, which indicates some of the measures are in 3/4 time while others are in 4/4 time.

In conducting these unusual rhythms, the leader will use the pattern of the time signature given in each part of the song. Conceivably, he may be conducting a measure of four beats immediately followed by a measure of only three beats. Such an arrangement, however, is very rare in hymns. A careful examination of each song prior to its use will reveal any irregularities or unusual rhythmic structures. Always, he should familiarize himself thoroughly with each song—its rhythm, tempo, mood, and message.

1. *Combination of Triple and Quadruple Rhythms*

We present here three songs which utilize in different ways some of the unusual measure rhythms. In each we shall use the simple triple and quadruple beat patterns.

"I Will Sing the Wondrous Story"

A careful study of this song will reveal the stanzas to be in 3/4 rhythm while the refrain is in 4/4 rhythm. The director will therefore conduct three beats to each measure for the stanzas and change to four beats to each measure for the refrain. He will alternate between 3/4 rhythm for all the stanzas and 4/4 rhythm for the refrain.

At the beginning of the refrain we encounter a three-note pickup, which is in triplet form. A triplet simply means that three notes are sung or played to the time of the basic beat note. In this case a quarter note is basic. Ordinarily, a quarter note equals two eighth notes, but it is possible to compress three eighth notes into one beat in triplet form. When a triplet is used, however, it always appears with a figure 3 written above or below the group.

The refrain uses some tied notes and accompanying rhythm parts in the men's voices. In conducting the refrain, the expression hand will sustain the ties and the lead hand will beat out the rhythm as it gestures to the men for each entrance. As the end of a tie is reached, both the expression and lead hands will sweep outward to indicate the release and then follow through on an upbeat which leads into the next measure. Practice this song a number of times in order to master the rhythm changes, ties, voice entrances, and measure accents.

"Love Is the Theme" (Ex. 39)

The time signature in this song is 4/4 in the stanzas and 3/4 in the refrain. We use the simple four-beat pattern, then the simple three-beat pattern, alternating at the beginning of each stanza and the refrain. The song leader should give special attention to the accents of the measures in order to improve the rhythmic flow. Special effects in the refrain may be achieved by asking a few of the sopranos to sing the small top notes which appear above the melody line.

"It May Be at Morn" (Ex. 40)

Here we have a most unusual time signature. The song is written both in 3/4 and 4/4 measure, and the signature is indicated by placing 3/4 4/4 at the beginning.

Study will reveal that the song begins on the upbeat 3 and continues through three measures of triple time before a measure of quadruple time occurs. This fourth measure is directed in a simple quadruple pattern. The second beat will be closed out with a short cutoff stroke; the hand will go outward for the rest on count 3 and then gesture in the singers on beat 4. Beat 3 demonstrates how a composer can use a rest to create a special effect in the music and to emphasize the words. In M.5 the song returns to three beats and continues to M.8 where the special effect, created through a change of time and the use of a rest, again occurs. The remainder of the song is in triple measure. In directing the refrain, it is possible to produce some startling effects through the building of a volume climax in the "hallelujahs." Work diligently on the expression possibilities, and use them in conducting this song.

100

EXERCISE 38.

I Will Sing the Wondrous Story

WONDROUS STORY. 8. 7. 8. 7. with Refrain

Francis H. Rowley, 1854-1952

Peter P. Bilhorn, 1861-1936

1. I will sing the won-drous sto - ry Of the Christ who died for me,
2. I was lost, but Je - sus found me, Found the sheep that went a - stray,
3. I was bruised, but Je - sus healed me; Faint was I from man-y a fall;
4. Days of dark - ness still come o'er me, Sor - row's paths I of - ten tread,
5. He will keep me till the riv - er Rolls its wa - ters at my feet;

How He left His home in glo - ry For the cross of Cal - va - ry.
Threw His lov - ing arms a - round me, Drew me back in - to His way.
Sight was gone, and fears pos-sessed me, But He freed me from them all.
But the Sav - iour still is with me; By His hand I'm safe - ly led.
Then He'll bear me safe - ly o - ver, Where the loved ones I shall meet.

REFRAIN

Yes, I'll sing........ the won - drous sto - - - ry Of the
Yes, I'll sing the won-drous sto - ry

Christ...... who died for me,......... Sing it with...... the saints in
Of the Christ who died for me, Sing it with

glo - - ry, Gath - ered by.......... the crys - tal sea...........
the saints in glo-ry, Gath - ered by the crys-tal sea.

Love Is the Theme

FISHER. 7. 7. 7. 9. with Refrain

ALBERT C. FISHER, 1886-1946   ALBERT C. FISHER, 1886-1946

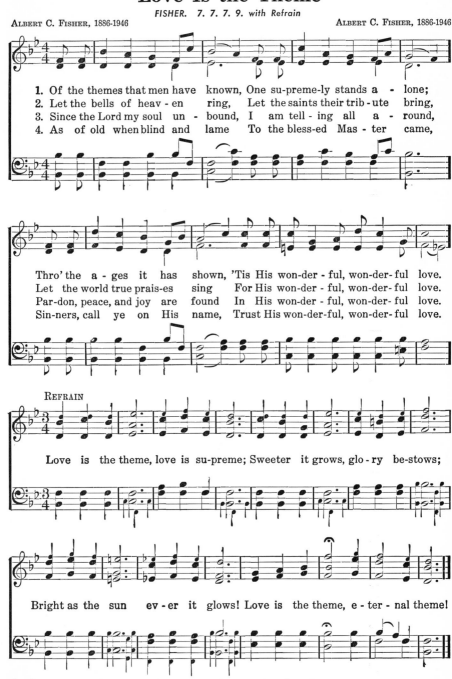

1. Of the themes that men have known, One su-preme-ly stands a - lone;
2. Let the bells of heav - en ring, Let the saints their trib - ute bring,
3. Since the Lord my soul un - bound, I am tell - ing all a - round,
4. As of old when blind and lame To the bless-ed Mas - ter came,

Thro' the a - ges it has shown, 'Tis His won-der - ful, won-der-ful love.
Let the world true prais-es sing For His won-der - ful, won-der-ful love.
Par-don, peace, and joy are found In His won-der - ful, won-der-ful love.
Sin-ners, call ye on His name, Trust His won-der-ful, won-der-ful love.

REFRAIN

Love is the theme, love is su-preme; Sweeter it grows, glo-ry be-stows;

Bright as the sun ev-er it glows! Love is the theme, e - ter - nal theme!

EXERCISE 40.

It May Be at Morn

CHRIST RETURNETH. *Irregular with Refrain*

H. L. TURNER

JAMES McGRANAHAN, 1840-1907

1. It may be at morn, when the day is a - wak - ing, When sun-light thro'
2. It may be at mid - day, it may be at twi-light, It may be, per-
3. While hosts cry ho - san - na, from heav-en de - scend-ing, With glo - ri - fied
4. Oh, joy! oh, de-light! should we go with-out dy - ing, No sick-ness, no

dark - ness and shad - ow is break-ing, That Je - sus will come in the
chance, that the black-ness of mid-night Will burst in - to light in the
saints and the an - gels at - tend-ing, With grace on His brow, like a
sad - ness, no dread and no cry - ing, Caught up thro' the clouds with our

ful - ness of glo - ry, To re - ceive from the world His own.
blaze of His glo - ry, When Je - sus re - ceives His own.
ha - lo of glo - ry, Will Je - sus re - ceive His own.
Lord in - to glo - ry, When Je - sus re - ceives His own.

REFRAIN

O Lord Je - sus, how long, how long Ere we shout the glad song, Christ re-

rit.

turn-eth! Hal - le - lu - jah! hal - le - lu - jah! A - men, hal - le - lu - jah! a - men.

2. *Combinations of Compound Measures*

Although the following songs are written in compound rhythms, we use the simple duple, triple, and quadruple patterns in directing them. Not one of the songs would be directed with multiple beats. Each one, moving at a rather fast tempo, calls for clear and precise conducting strokes.

"I Will Sing of My Redeemer"

Immediately the song leader will observe that the stanzas are in 9/8 rhythm and the refrain is in 12/8 rhythm. Reduced to simple patterns, the song would be directed in three beats for the stanzas and four beats for the refrain. In so doing, the song leader will notice a great similarity to "I Will Sing the Wondrous Story." The two songs, although different in time signatures, are directed and interpreted almost exactly in the same manner.

"Saved, Saved!"

This famous revival song is written in 12/8 and 6/8 time. The stanzas are directed in four beats and the refrain in two beats. The stanzas offer opportunity for intensity of tone through unison singing, but care should be exercised lest this intensity be lost by singing the song too slowly. The refrain is to be sung at the same tempo as the stanzas, but the change is made to a two-beat measure. Many directors like to develop a gradual *ritard* in the last score by changing to six beats in the third measure from the end, building all the while toward a climax on "saved, saved, saved!" conducted with one beat to each of the words.

"Ready"

The signature of "Ready" is 9/8 6/8. Careful study will reveal the third measure of each four-measure phrase to be in 6/8 time, although the remainder of the song is in 9/8 time. The song will be directed with the three-beat pattern except where the 6/8 measure occurs in each phrase. This measure will be directed in two-beat form. The song is devotional in nature and should be conducted with a modified expressive beat.

II. EXTENDED SONG FORMS

We have previously called attention to the fact that most hymns and gospel songs are constructed in four-measure phrases and usually contain sixteen measures. Of course some songs have fewer, and some have more, but the sixteen-measure song is the general form.

Some songs are extended beyond standard length, having been written for special uses. Some are twenty-four measures in length, some

EXERCISE 41.

I Will Sing of My Redeemer

MY REDEEMER. 8. 7. 8. 7. with Refrain

Philip P. Bliss, 1838-1876

James McGranahan, 1840-1907

1. I will sing of my Re-deem-er And His won-drous love to me;
2. I will tell the won-drous sto-ry, How my lost es-tate to save,
3. I will praise my dear Re-deem-er, His tri-um-phant power I'll tell,
4. I will sing of my Re-deem-er, And His heaven-ly love to me;

On the cru-el cross He suf-fered From the curse to set me free.
In His bound-less love and mer-cy, He the ran-som free-ly gave.
How the vic-to-ry He giv-eth O-ver sin and death and hell.
He from death to life hath brought me, Son of God, with Him to be.

REFRAIN

Sing, oh, sing............ of my Re-deem-er, With His
Sing, oh, sing of my Re-deem-er, Sing, oh, sing of my Re-deem-er, With His

blood...... He pur-chased me;........ On the cross........ He sealed my
blood He purchased me, With His blood He purchased me; On the cross He sealed my pardon, On the

par-don, Paid the debt.......... and made me free........
cross He sealed my par-don, Paid the debt and made me free, and made me free.

EXERCISE 42.

Saved, Saved!

RAPTURE. 9. 6. 9. 8. with Refrain

JACK P. SCHOLFIELD, 1882-

JACK P. SCHOLFIELD, 1882-

1. I've found a friend who is all to me, His love is ev-er true; .... I love to tell how He lift-ed me, And what His grace can do for you. ....

2. He saves me from ev-ery sin and harm, Se-cures my soul each day; .... I'm lean-ing strong on His might-y arm; I know He'll guide me all the way. ....

3. When poor and need-y and all a-lone, In love He said to me, ... "Come un-to Me and I'll lead you home, To live with Me e-ter-nal-ly." ....

REFRAIN

Saved...... by His power di-vine, Saved...... to new life sub-lime!
Saved by His power,   Saved to new life,

Life now is sweet and my joy is com-plete, For I'm saved, saved, saved!

© Copyright 1911 by Robert H. Coleman. Renewal 1939, Broadman Press

EXERCISE 43.

Ready

TILLMAN. C. M. with Refrain

Anonymous

CHARLES D. TILLMAN, 1861-1943

1. Read-y to suf-fer grief or pain, Read-y to stand the test;
2. Read-y to go, read-y to bear, Read-y to watch and pray;
3. Read-y to speak, read-y to think, Read-y with heart and brain;
4. Read-y to speak, read-y to warn, Read-y o'er souls to yearn;

Read-y to stay at home and send Oth-ers, if He sees best.
Read-y to stand a-side and give, Till He shall clear the way.
Read-y to stand where He sees fit, Read-y to stand the strain.
Read-y in life, read-y in death, Read-y for His re-turn.

REFRAIN

Read-y to go, read-y to stay, Read-y my place to fill;

Read-y for serv-ice, low-ly or great, Read-y to do His will.

107

Stand Up, Stand Up for Jesus

GEIBEL. 7. 6. 7. 6. D. with Refrain

GEORGE DUFFIELD, JR., 1818-1888   ADAM GEIBEL, 1855-1933

In unison

1. Stand up, stand up for Je - sus, Ye sol - diers of the cross;
2. Stand up, stand up for Je - sus, The trum - pet call o - bey;
3. Stand up, stand up for Je - sus, Stand in His strength a - lone;
4. Stand up, stand up for Je - sus, The strife will not be long;

Lift high His roy - al ban - ner, It must not suf - fer loss:
Forth to the might - y con - flict, In this His glo - rious day:
The arm of flesh will fail you, Ye dare not trust your own:
This day the noise of bat - tle, The next, the vic - tor's song:

From vic - t'ry un - to vic - t'ry His ar - my shall He lead,
Ye that are men now serve Him A - gainst un - num-bered foes;
Put on the gos - pel ar - mor, Each piece put on with prayer;
To him that o - ver - com - eth A crown of life shall be;

Till ev - 'ry foe is van - quished, And Christ is Lord in - deed.
Let cour - age rise with dan - ger, And strength to strength op - pose.
Where du - ty calls or dan - ger, Be nev - er want - ing there.
He, with the King of glo - ry, Shall reign e - ter - nal - ly.

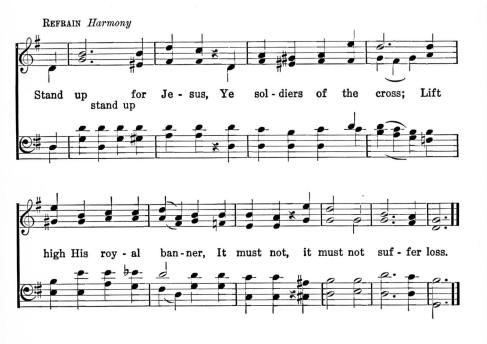

Stand up   for   Je - sus, Ye   sol - diers of   the   cross; Lift
        stand up

high His   roy - al   ban - ner, It must not, it must not suf - fer loss.

thirty-two, others even longer. Almost without exception, however, the number of measures is a multiple of four.

As we reach the close of our text, we include seven songs in extended form for the song leader's study and practice as he grows in knowledge and develops his ability to lead group singing. Each song is in extended form and should be studied carefully. By giving close attention to detail, interpretation, phrasing, and the prudent use of many gestures and patterns learned thus far, the song leader should be able to find real joy and a sense of accomplishment in leading each of the songs. And he will undoubtedly wish to use his new knowledge and skills as steppingstones to greater achievement in the field of conducting.

The Master Hath Come

ASH GROVE. 12. 11. 12. 11. D.

Sarah Doudney, 1841-1926

Welsh Melody

1. The Mas-ter hath come, and He calls us to fol-low The track of the
foot-prints He leaves on our way; Far o-ver the moun-tain and
through the deep hol-low, The path leads us on to the man-sions of day:
The Mas-ter hath called us, the children who fear Him, Who march 'neath Christ's

2. The Mas-ter hath called us; the road may be drear-y, And dan-gers and
sor-rows are strewn on the track; But God's Ho-ly Spir-it shall
com-fort the wea-ry; We fol-low the Sav-iour and can-not turn back;
The Mas-ter hath called us: though doubt and temp-ta-tion May com-pass our

3. The Mas-ter hath called us, in life's ear-ly morn-ing, With spir-its as
fresh as the dew on the sod: We turn from the world, with its
smiles and its scorn-ing, To cast in our lot with the peo-ple of God:
The Mas-ter hath called us, His sons and His daugh-ters, We plead for His

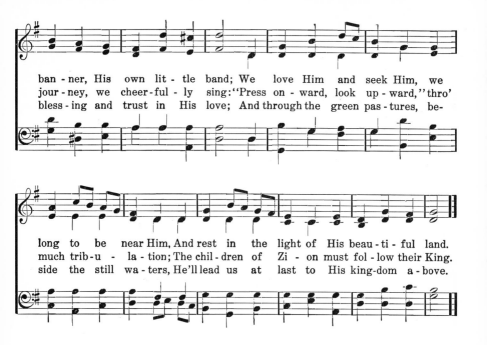

ban - ner, His own lit - tle band; We love Him and seek Him, we
jour - ney, we cheer - ful - ly sing: "Press on - ward, look up - ward," thro'
bless - ing and trust in His love; And through the green pas - tures, be-

long to be near Him, And rest in the light of His beau - ti - ful land.
much trib - u - la - tion; The chil - dren of Zi - on must fol - low their King.
side the still wa - ters, He'll lead us at last to His king-dom a - bove.

FOR FURTHER STUDY

1. Procure a copy of *Selections for the Revival Choir* (Broadman Press). Study the hymn arrangements and practice conducting each.

2. Develop an evaluation sheet, listing those things you consider essential to superior song leading. Organize the qualities in such a manner as to be able to check quickly and accurately the work of any song leader you observe. Use the sheet.

3. If you are not presently serving as a song leader, offer your services and put into actual practice that which you have learned.

4. Encourage your church to maintain classes for song leaders and for training others for service in the Music Ministry.

The Spacious Firmament

CREATION. *L. M. D.*

JOSEPH ADDISON, 1672-1719

From *The Creation*
FRANZ J. HAYDN, 1732-1809

1. The spa-cious firm-a-ment on high, With all the blue e - the - real sky,
2. Soon as the eve-ning shades pre-vail, The moon takes up the won-drous tale,
3. What tho' in sol-emn si - lence all Move round the dark ter-res-trial ball?

And spangled heav'ns a shin - ing frame, Their great O - rig-i - nal pro-claim:
And night-ly, to the lis-tening earth, Re - peats the sto-ry of her birth;
What tho' no re - al voice nor sound A - mid the ra-diant orbs be found?

Th' un-wea-ried sun, from day to day, Does his Cre - a - tor's power dis-play,
While all the stars that round her burn, And all the plan-ets in their turn,
In rea-son's ear they all re-joice, And ut - ter forth a glo - rious voice,

And pub - lish-es to ev - ery land The work of an al-mighty hand.
Con-firm the tid - ings as they roll, And spread the truth from pole to pole.
For - ev - er sing - ing, as they shine, "The hand that made us is di-vine." A-MEN.

Praise Ye the Father

CHARLES GOUNOD
Arranged by B. B. MCKINNEY

Praise ye the Fa - ther! Let ev - ery heart give thanks to Him!

Praise ye the Fa - ther, Who is ev - er kind and mer - ci - ful!

Praise ye the Fa - ther, Who not - eth ev - ery spar - row's fall!

O King of Glo - ry! Let all earth pro - claim Thy maj - es - ty!

Sing Of Him sing praise, of the Lord, Ev - ery voice pro - claim His power!

Arr. Copyright, 1940, by The Sunday School Board of the Southern Baptist Convention.

to the Son, and Ho - ly Spir - it! Praise Him, ev - ery

na - tion, All the earth shall re - joice in Him!.......... Praise the Fa-ther!

Glo - ry to the Lord our King! Glo - ry to His ev - er-

last - ing name! Let all earth be glad, re - joic - ing in His love,

Oh, praise ye the Lord! praise ye the Lord!

EXERCISE 48.

Lead On, Lead On

B. B. McKinney

B. B. McKinney

1. Lead on, O King of Glo - ry, We will fol - low, fol - low Thee,
2. Lead on, O King of Glo - ry, We will sing the glad re - frain,
3. Lead on, O King of Glo - ry, Lead on for truth and right,

Thy crim - son ban - ner o - ver us Shall a sign of tri - umph be;
Lead on, O Great De - liv - er - er, O - ver all the world's do - main;
Lift high Thy cross e - ter - nal, Lead on, O Prince of Light;

Thou e - ter - nal Christ of Cal - va - ry, Lead us on from sea to sea,
We have heard Thy call to loy - al - ty, We will strive to set men free,
Let re - deem - ing love per - vade the world, Let its ban - ner be un - furled,

Till the day is done, And the crown is won, Lead on, lead on, lead on!
For the cause of right We will stand and fight, Lead us on, O God of Might.
Till the strife shall cease In a calm re - lease, Lead us on, O Prince of Peace.

Chorus Parts

EXERCISE 49.

Hallelujah for the Cross

HORATIUS BONAR, Alt.   JAMES MCGRANAHAN

1. The cross it stand-eth fast, Hal - le - lu - jah! hal - le - lu - jah! De - fy - ing
2. It is the old cross still, Hal - le - lu - jah! hal - le - lu - jah! Its tri-umph
3. 'Twas here the debt was paid, Hal - le - lu - jah! hal - le - lu - jah! Our sins on

ev - ery blast, Hal-le - lu-jah, hal - le - lu-jah! The winds of hell have blown, The
let us tell, Hal-le - lu-jah, hal - le - lu-jah! The grace of God here shown Thro'
Je - sus laid, Hal-le - lu-jah, hal - le - lu-jah! So round the cross we sing Of

cresc.

world its hate hath shown, Yet it is not overthrown, Hal-le-lu-jah for the cross!
Christ the bless-ed Son, Who did for sin a - tone, Hal-le-lu-jah for the cross!
Christ our of - fer - ing, Of Christ our liv-ing King, Hal-le-lu-jah for the cross!

OBBLIGATO DUET SOP. (or TEN.) and ALTO

Hal - le - lu - jah,   hal - le - lu - jah,   Hal - le-

SOPRANO & ALTO*

CHORUS mp   Hal - le - lu - jah,   hal - le - lu - jah, Hal - le-

*If desired, the Soprano and Alto may sing the upper staff, omitting the middle staff.

EXERCISE 49. (continued)

lu - jah for the cross!   Hal - le - lu - jah,

lu - jah for the cross, hal - le - lu - jah for the cross!   Hal - le - lu - jah,

hal - le - lu - jah,   It shall nev - er   suf - fer   loss!

hal - le - lu - jah, It shall nev - er suf - fer, nev-er suf - fer loss!

FULL CHORUS

*Hal - le - lu - jah,   hal - le - lu - jah,   Hal - le - lu - jah   for   the cross!

cresc.   ff

Hal - le - lu - jah,   hal - le - lu - jah,   It shall nev - er   suf - fer   loss!

*For a final ending, all the voices may sing the melody in unison through the last eight
measures—the instrument playing the harmony.

God So Loved the World

JOHN STAINER

God so loved the world, God so loved the world, that He gave His
world, that He

on - ly be-got-ten Son, that who-so be-liev-eth, be-liev-eth in Him should not

per - ish, should not per - ish, but have ev - er - last - ing life. For God sent not His

Son in - to the world to con-demn the world, God sent not His Son in - to the

world to con-demn the world, But that the world thro' Him might be sav - ed.

God so loved the world, God so loved the world, that He gave His
world that He

on - ly be - got - ten Son, that who - so be - liev - eth, be - liev - eth in Him

should not per - ish, should not per - ish, but have ev - er - last - ing

life, ev - er - last - ing, ev - er - last - ing life.
ev - er - last - ing life, ev - er - last - ing life.

God so loved the world, God so loved the world, God so loved the world.

Questions for Review and Written Work

Chapter 1

1. Enumerate and explain some of the qualifications a person should possess in order to become a good song leader.

2. In what ways do attire, manner, enthusiasm, sincerity, musicianship, and imagination contribute to successful song leading?

3. What are some of the techniques which you consider essential to good style in song leading?

Chapter 2

4. Name and explain the three elements that make up music.

5. Define the following: (1) measure, (2) clef, (3) time signature, (4) beats, (5) notes, (6) rests, (7) accent.

6. What is the "field of beating"? What is its relation to the various patterns of conducting?

7. Should an accompanist understand song leading? Why?

Chapter 3

8. What are some of the devices that can be used to develop clarity in song leading?

9. Describe the two-beat diagram and the best way to vary it in order to conduct the different types of songs in duple measure.

10. Describe briefly the functions of (1) the lead hand, (2) the expression hand.

Chapter 4

11. Draw both the simple and modified forms of the three-beat pattern. Explain why each is used.

12. Describe the *hold* and how you would conduct it on the first beat; second beat; last beat.

13. How does the message of a song help to determine the conducting pattern?

QUESTIONS FOR REVIEW AND WRITTEN WORK

Chapter 5

14. Draw the diagrams for simple and modified four-beat measure, and explain the functions of each.

15. Name and explain the uses of the expression hand in conducting.

16. Write out your interpretation of the song, "It Is Well with My Soul," and tell how you would conduct it.

Chapter 6

17. Draw both the German and Italian style patterns for six-beat measure, and tell which you prefer and why.

18. Explain how and why we reduce a six-beat measure to compound duple measure.

19. Explain how you would interpret "Sweet Peace, the Gift of God's Love."

Chapter 7

20. Draw the nine-beat diagram and explain how it can be reduced to a triple-measure pattern.

21. Write out your interpretation of "Blessed Assurance, Jesus Is Mine," and explain how you would conduct it.

22. Draw the twelve-beat diagram; also the compound quadruple diagram. Explain how they are related.

Chapter 8

23. Tell how it is possible to make conducting meaningful by conducting words and phrases.

24. Write out your full interpretation of "Sun of My Soul."

25. Enumerate and explain some factors which will help in the interpretation of hymns.

26. What physical factors should be checked by the song leader? Explain how each has a bearing on the singing of the people.

Chapter 9

27. Explain why unusual time signatures are used by composers.

28. Write out your interpretation of the song, "It May Be at Morn."

29. What is extended song form? How can it help you to become a better conductor?

SONG LEADING